How to Get a Job NOW!

Six Easy Steps to Getting a Good Job

J. Michael Farr

*America's Foremost
Career & Job Search Author*

How to Get a Job NOW!
Six Easy Steps to Getting a Good Job

> **Other books by this author:**
> *The Very Quick Job Search*
> *The Quick Resume & Cover Letter Book*
> *The Quick Salary & Negotiation Book*
> *Getting the Job You Really Want*
> *The Right Job for You*
> *The Work Book*
> *A Young Person's Guide to Getting and Keeping a Good Job*
> *America's Fastest Growing Jobs*
> *America's Top Jobs® for College Graduates*
> *America's Top Jobs® for People Without a Four-Year Degree*
> *America's Top White-Collars Jobs*
> *America's Top Medical, Education, & Human Services Jobs®*

Library of Congress Cataloging-in-Publication Data
Farr, J. Michael.
  How to get a job now! : six easy steps to getting a better job /
J. Michael Farr
    p.   cm.
    ISBN 1-56370-290-8
    1. Job hunting. I. Title
HF5382.7.F368   1996   96-38075
650.14--dc21   CIP

We have been careful to provide accurate information throughout this book, but it is possible that errors and omissions have been introduced. Please consider this in making any career plans or other important decisions. Trust your own judgment above all else and in all things.

JIST Works, Inc.
8902 Otis Avenue • Indianapolis, IN 46216
Phone: 1-800-648-JIST   Fax: 1-800-JIST-FAX
E-mail: JISTWorks@aol.com
World Wide Web Address: http://www.jist.com/jist

ISBN: 1-56730-290-8

Acknowledgments

The more you give away, the more you get back in return. . . .

I've written more than 20 books on career and job search topics, but I've never written an acknowledgments page. The truth is, I don't know where to begin in thanking everyone who has helped me over the years, but this is a start:

- ☼ *My Mom:* She's 88 years young now and loves to show off my books to relatives and anyone else nearby. I love her dearly, and she continues to inspire me. Anna is also personally responsible for rearranging my books to face out in bookstores throughout southwest Florida, should you ever wonder about that. Hi mom!

- ☼ *My Dad:* He modeled the work ethic I own, and the persistence (there were five kids in the family). He retired after 29 years with the same employer, a remarkable record. Thanks for being there. Oh, and I'm sorry for all the trouble I caused you as a teenager, including all those tools you couldn't find. . . .

- ☼ *Sandra:* We've been married 28 years now (or maybe 29), and I still can't get her to do what I want. But she's been there through all of my career changes and most of my life. I still like spending time with her–can you imagine? Thanks for everything.

- ☼ *Sister William Mary:* My teacher in grades 6, 7, and 8. She forced me to write as a punishment for bad behavior. I still have bad behaviors and I still write. Thanks for being a good teacher.

- ☼ *A.J. Nania:* My freshman-year English professor at Notre Dame. He taught me to write things short and long (short is harder, I learned, and takes longer per page) and to understand eighth-grade grammar (I passed).

☼ *My family:* I have two good children (now young adults), great brothers and sisters, aunts and uncles, nieces and nephews. We even like getting together.

☼ *Everyone else:* I have a very long list of people who have helped me along the way, including good friends, the good people I work with, the many job seekers from whom I have learned so much, and so many others.

Thanks.

Foreword

I have been teaching job seeking skills for many years.
Sometimes, I have had just a few hours to teach an
individual or group *the* most important things to know in
order to get a job. This has forced me to think about what
is most important to know, if time is short.

If I had only a few hours to teach you the best ways to get a
better job in less time, I would cover the techniques
presented in this book. You can read it and do all the
activities in just a few hours.

You could read this book in a morning and conduct a more
effective job search that very afternoon. And you may find
this book is all you need.

Of course, there is more to know about career planning
and job seeking than is contained in this book. I've written
more detailed books, and there are scores of other books on
the topic. But these are the basics. If you use the
techniques–not just read about them, *use them*–the odds
are good that you will reduce the time it takes to find a job.
And you are likely to find a better job than you would have
otherwise.

I wish you well.

Mike Farr

Table of Contents

Introduction 1

Changing Jobs and Careers Is Often Healthy 2
But Not Just Any Job Should Do—Nor Any Job Search 3
Six Steps for a Quick Job Search 4

1 Identify Your Skills and Develop a "Skills Language" to Describe Yourself 7

Three Types of Skills 7
    Self-Management Skills 8
    Transferable Skills 11
    Job-Related Skills 15

2 Define Your Ideal Job (You Can Always Compromise Later) 17

Your Ideal Job 21
Set a Specific Job Objective 22
The Top 250 Jobs in the U.S. Workforce 23

3 Use Methods That Reduce Your Job Search Time 35

Traditional Job Search Methods Are Not Very Effective 35
The Two Job Search Methods That Work Best 38
    Method 1: Develop a Network of Contacts
    in Five Easy Steps 39
    Method 2: Contact Employers Directly 41
    JIST Cards: Effective "Mini-Resumes" 42

4 Redefine What "Counts" as an Interview, Then Get Two a Day 47

Make Your Job Search a Full-Time Job 48
    Spend at Least 25 Hours a Week Looking for a Job 49
    Create a Daily Schedule 50

5 Quick Tips That Make a Big Difference in the Interview 53

The First Impression May Be the Only Impression You Make ... 54
    Quick Tips for Creating a Good Impression 54
A Traditional Interview Is Not a Friendly Exchange 55
How to Answer Tough Interview Questions 56
    The Three-Step Process for Answering Questions 57
Salary Negotiations—A Few Techniques to Help You
Earn Thousands of Dollars a Minute 59
Close the Interview Effectively 60

6 Follow Up On All Contacts 63

Thank-You Notes Make a Difference 64
Use Job Lead Cards to Organize Your Contacts 65

7 Resumes: Write a Simple One Now and a Better One Later 67

Tips for Creating a Superior Resume 68
Chronological Resumes 70
    Tips for Writing a Simple Chronological Resume 70
    Tips for an Improved Chronological Resume 73
Skills and Combination Resumes 75
The Quick Job Search Review 79

Appendix A: Essential Job Search Data Worksheet 81

Appendix B: More Sample Resumes 91

Appendix C: Some Tips for Coping With Job Loss 109

Problems You May Encounter 109
Adjusting 110
Keep Healthy 111
Family Issues 112
    Helping Children 112
Coping with Stress 113
    Keep Your Spirits Up 115
    Overcoming Depression 116
    Sources of Professional Help 117
Managing Your Finances 117
    Apply for Benefits Without Delay 118
    Prepare Now to Stretch Your Money 118
    Review Your Health Coverage 121

Appendix D: Bibliography—Sources of Job Leads and Other Information ...123

Career Planning, Job Seeking, Resumes, and Career Success 124
    Job Seeking and Interviewing 124
    Resumes and Cover Letters 125
    Education, Self-Employment, and Starting a Business 126
Information on Occupations and Industries 127
Information on Specific Organizations 129
    Professional and Trade Associations 131
    Newspapers 131
    Networking 132
Computer Software 132

Introduction

You will soon discover this is not simply a job search book. It includes career planning advice, suggestions for surviving unemployment, and other information that is not just "how to get a job."

These "other" topics can be quite important to you, though you might be tempted to skip over them. I especially urge you to review the career planning material, even if you have a fairly clear job objective. Skipping it will leave you ill-prepared to conduct an effective job search.

I say this because I firmly believe you should have a strong sense of what you have to offer and what you really want to do *before* you go looking for a job. I know this is not always easy. But time spent on career planning will help you clarify what you *really* want. Even if you don't get it now, you will have set a steady long-term goal.

Do the activities, please.
While this book will teach you techniques to find a better job in less time, job seeking requires you to act, *not just learn. So consider what you can do to put the techniques to work for you. Do the activities. Create a daily plan. Get more interviews. Today, not tomorrow! You see, the sooner and harder you get to work on your job search, the shorter it is likely to be.*

There is also a job search payoff for doing your career planning homework. For example, if you do the activities to *identify* your key skills, then you can *tell an employer about them.* Emphasizing these skills in an interview, in just the right way, can give you an enormous advantage over the competition. Trust me on this. It is worth the time.

As for the job search techniques, they are short and to the point. But don't confuse their brevity with their effectiveness. I've spent more than 20 years developing techniques to reduce the time it takes to find a job–and these are the techniques presented in this book. They have been proven to reduce the time it takes to get a job *by half or more.* Since the average length of unemployment varies from 12 to 16 weeks (depending on the unemployment rate), anything that reduces that time is worth a lot of money to you.

Changing Jobs and Careers Is Often Healthy

Most of us were told from an early age that each career move must be up–involving more money, responsibility, and prestige. Yet research indicates that people change careers for many other reasons as well.

In a poll conducted by the Gallup Organization for the National Occupational Information Coordinating Committee, 44 percent of the working adults surveyed expected to be in different jobs within three years–a very high turnover rate. Yet only 41 percent of those anticipating a change had a definite plan for charting their careers.

Logical, ordered careers are closely associated with increasing levels of education. For example, while 25 percent of the high school dropouts in the survey said they had taken the only job available, this was true for only 8 percent of those with at least some college.

But is occupational stability always healthy? Many adult developmental psychologists believe occupational change not only is normal but may even be necessary for sound adult growth and development. It is common to reconsider occupational roles during your 20s, 30s, and 40s—even in the absence of economic pressure to do so.

One viewpoint is that a healthy occupational change is one that allows some previously undeveloped talent or interest to emerge. The change may be as natural as a move from clerk to supervisor, or as drastic as one from professional musician to airline pilot. Although there's always risk when you make a change, reasonable risks are healthy and can even raise your self-esteem.

But Not Just Any Job Should Do—Nor Any Job Search

Whether you are seeking similar work in another setting or changing careers, you need a workable plan to find the right job. This book will give you the information you need to help you find a good job quickly.

The techniques are based on my years of experience in helping people find good jobs (not just any job) in less time. The career decision-making section will help you consider the major issues involved in choosing a career. The job-seeking skills are ones that have been proven to reduce the amount of time it takes to find a good job.

QUIP

Good news for those who do their homework! *Most people spend more time watching TV each week than they spend on career planning in an entire year—and fewer than 10 percent of all job seekers even read a book on job seeking. While this is a big problem for them, it is good news for you, since knowing even a little more than the next person can give you a big advantage in the job search and in life!*

Of course, more thorough books have been written on job-seeking techniques, and you might want to look at one or more to obtain additional information. (A list of such books is included at the back of this book.) But, short as it is, this book *does* present the basic skills to find a good job in less time. The techniques work!

Six Steps for a Quick Job Search

You can't just read about getting a job, you have to go out and get interviews! And the best way to get a job is to make a job out of getting a job.

From my years of working with job seekers, I have identified six simple steps that make a big difference in a job search. If you focus on doing each of these things reasonably well, you are far more likely to get a better job in less time.

The Six Steps for a Quick Job Search

Step 1: *Know your skills*

Step 2: *Have a clear job objective*

Step 3: *Know where and how to look for job leads*

Step 4: *Spend at least 25 hours a week looking*

Step 5: *Get two interviews a day*

Step 6: *Follow up on all contacts*

Each of these steps is covered in this book. Some take more pages to cover than others, but they are all there and they are all important.

With that said, let's get started!

Chapter 1

Identify Your Skills and Develop a "Skills Language" to Describe Yourself

A recent survey of employers revealed that 90 percent of the people who came in for interviews did not present the skills they had to do the jobs they sought. They could not answer the basic question, "Why should I hire you?"

Knowing your skills is essential to do well in an interview. This same knowledge is important in deciding what type of job you will enjoy and do well. Identifying your skills is an essential part of a successful career plan or job search.

Three Types of Skills

When you say the word "skills" most people think of job-related skills, such as using a computer. But we all have other kinds of skills that are important for success on a job and that are very important to employers. The Skills Triad below presents skills in three groups. These groupings provide a useful way to consider skills for our purposes.

We all have thousands of skills. Consider the many skills required to do even a simple thing like ride a bike or bake a cake. Of all the skills you have, employers want to know about certain key skills you have to do the job they need done. You must clearly identify these key skills, then emphasize them in an interview.

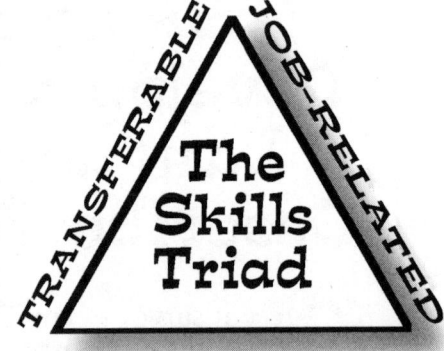

Let's review these three types of skills and identify those that are most important to you.

Self-Management Skills

Write down in the box titled "Your 'Good Worker' Traits" on the next page three things about yourself that you think make you a good worker.

Your "Good Worker" Traits

1. _____

2. _____

3. _____

The things you just wrote down are among the most important things an employer should know about you! They have to do with your basic personality–your ability to adapt to a new environment. They are some of the most important things to emphasize in an interview, yet most job seekers don't realize their importance and don't mention them.

Review the Self-Management Skills Checklist below and put a checkmark beside any skills you have. The Key Self-Management Skills are those that employers find particularly important. If any of these Key Self-Management Skills apply to you, mentioning them in an interview can help you greatly.

Self-Management Skills Checklist

Key Self-Management Skills

____	accept supervision	____	hard worker
____	get along with coworkers	____	honest
____	get things done on time	____	productive
____	good attendance	____	punctual

Other Self-Management Skills

____ able to coordinate	____ modest
____ ambitious	____ motivated
____ assertive	____ natural
____ capable	____ open-minded
____ cheerful	____ optimistic
____ competent	____ original
____ complete assignments	____ patient
____ conscientious	____ persistent
____ creative	____ physically strong
____ dependable	____ practice new skills
____ discreet	____ reliable
____ eager	____ resourceful
____ efficient	____ responsible
____ energetic	____ self-confident
____ enthusiastic	____ sense of humor
____ expressive	____ sincere
____ flexible	____ solve problems
____ formal	____ spontaneous
____ friendly	____ steady
____ good-natured	____ tactful
____ helpful	____ take pride in work
____ humble	____ tenacious
____ imaginative	____ thrifty
____ independent	____ trustworthy
____ industrious	____ versatile
____ informal	____ well-organized
____ intelligent	
____ intuitive	**Others:**
____ loyal	_____
____ mature	_____
____ methodical	_____
	_____

When you are done, circle the five skills you think are most important and list them in the box below.

Your Top Five Self-Management Skills

1. _____

2. _____

3. _____

4. _____

5. _____

Too good to be true?

It's okay to tell the truth, even if it makes you feel good. Using your new "skills language" may be uncomfortable at first, but it tells employers what they need to know in an interview.

Transferable Skills

We all have skills that can transfer from one job or career to another. For example, the ability to organize events can be used in a variety of jobs and is essential for success in certain occupations. Your mission is to find a job that requires the skills you have and enjoy using.

In the following list, put a checkmark beside the skills you have. You may have used them in a previous job or in a nonwork setting.

Transferable Skills Checklist

Key Transferable Skills

____ instruct others
____ manage money
____ manage people
____ meet deadlines
____ meet the public
____ negotiate
____ organize/manage projects
____ speak in public
____ written communication skills

Skills Working with Things

____ assemble things
____ build things
____ drive, operate vehicles
____ good with hands
____ observe/inspect
____ operate tools, machines
____ repair things
____ use complex equipment

Skills Working with Data

____ analyze data
____ audit records
____ budget
____ calculate/compute
____ check for accuracy
____ classify things
____ compare
____ compile
____ count
____ detail-oriented
____ evaluate
____ investigate
____ keep financial records
____ locate information
____ manage money
____ observe/inspect
____ record facts
____ research
____ synthesize
____ take inventory

Skills Working with People

____ administer
____ advise

_____ care for
_____ coach
_____ confront others
_____ counsel people
_____ demonstrate
_____ diplomatic
_____ help others
_____ instruct
_____ interview people
_____ kind
_____ listen
_____ negotiate
_____ outgoing

_____ patient
_____ perceptive
_____ persuade
_____ pleasant
_____ sensitive
_____ sociable
_____ supervise
_____ tactful
_____ tolerant
_____ tough
_____ trusting
_____ understanding

Skills Working with Words, Ideas

_____ articulate
_____ communicate
_____ verbally
_____ correspond with
        others
_____ create new ideas
_____ design
_____ edit

_____ ingenious
_____ inventive
_____ library research
_____ logical
_____ speak in public
_____ remember
        information
_____ write clearly

Leadership Skills

_____ arrange social
        functions
_____ competitive
_____ decisive
_____ delegate
_____ direct others
_____ explain things
_____ influence others
_____ initiate new tasks

_____ make decisions
_____ manage or direct
        others
_____ mediate problems
_____ motivate people
_____ negotiate
        agreements
_____ plan events
_____ results-oriented

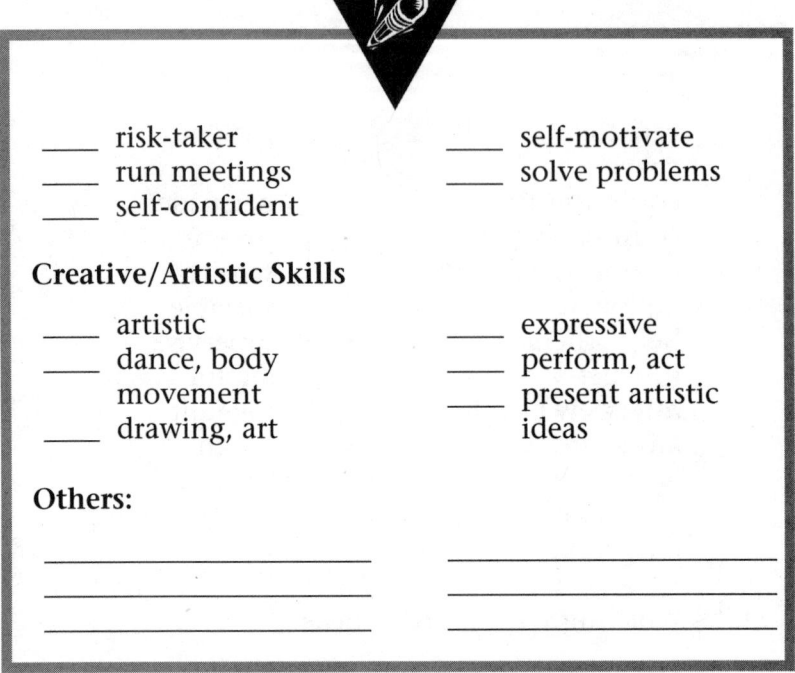

_____ risk-taker
_____ run meetings
_____ self-confident

_____ self-motivate
_____ solve problems

Creative/Artistic Skills

_____ artistic
_____ dance, body
      movement
_____ drawing, art

_____ expressive
_____ perform, act
_____ present artistic
      ideas

Others:

_____
_____
_____

_____
_____

When you are finished, identify the five transferable skills that are most important for you to use in your next job and list them in the box below.

Your Top Five Transferable Skills

1. _____
2. _____
3. _____
4. _____
5. _____

Job-Related Skills

Job-content or job-related skills are those you need to do a particular job. A carpenter, for example, must know how to use various tools and be familiar with a variety of tasks related to that job.

You may already have a good idea of the type of job you want. If so, it might be easy for you to identify which job-related skills to emphasize in an interview. But I recommend that you complete at least two other items in this book first:

1. Complete the material in the next chapter that helps you define your job objective. Doing so will help you clarify just what sort of a job you want and allow you to better select those skills that best support it.

2. If you have not already done so, complete the Essential Job Search Data Worksheet in Appendix A. It will give you several specific skills and accomplishments to consider.

Once you have done these two things, come back and complete the box below. Include the job-related skills you have that you would most like to use in your next job.

> **QUIP**
>
> **It's a hassle, but:**
> *Completing the worksheet in Appendix A will help you understand what you are good at— and to remember examples of when you did things well. This will be tremendously valuable to you in the interview, when those few things you say matter so much. Look at the worksheet now, and promise to do it tonight. Really. Then review the skills worksheets in this section and make any needed changes.*

Your Top Five Job-Related Skills

1. _____

2. _____

3. _____

4. _____

5. _____

C·h·a·p·t·e·r

2

Define Your Ideal Job (You Can Always Compromise Later)

Too many people begin looking for a job without having a good idea of exactly what they are looking for. Before you go looking for *"a"* job, I suggest you first define exactly what it is you really want–*THE* job. Most people think a job objective is the same as a job title, but it isn't. You need to consider other elements of what makes a job satisfying for you. Then, later, you can decide what that job is called and what industry it might be in.

Eight Factors to Consider
in Defining Your Ideal Job

Below are eight things you should think about when you are defining your ideal job. Once you know what you want, your task becomes finding a job that is as close to your ideal as possible.

1. **Which Skills Do You Want to Use?**
    From the skills lists in Chapter 1, select the five skills you most enjoy using and want to use in your next job.

    1. _____
    2. _____
    3. _____
    4. _____
    5. _____

2. **What Special Knowledge Do You Have?**
    Maybe you know how to fix radios, keep accounting records, or cook gourmet meals. Write down the things you know about from school, training, hobbies, family experiences, volunteer work, and other sources. One or more of these abilities could make you a perfect candidate in the right job setting.

    _____
    _____
    _____
    _____
    _____

3. What Kind of People Do You Want to Work With?

Do you like to work with aggressive, hard workers or laid-back folks? Creative types or down-to-earth pragmatists? Engineers or musicians? Old folks or young? Give some thought to the people you like to work with, because your coworkers will greatly influence the work environment.

_____

_____

_____

_____

_____

4. What Kind of Work Environment Do You Prefer?

Do you want to work inside or outside? Is it important to you to be in a quiet place, a busy place, or a clean place? Do you need to have a window with a nice view? List the things that are important to you.

_____

_____

_____

_____

_____

5. Where Do You Want Your Next Job to Be?

Do you need to work near a bus line? Close to a child-care center? Do you want to stay in a

particular city or region, or are you willing to move? If you are open to living or working anywhere, what would your ideal community be like?

_____

_____

_____

_____

_____

6. **How Much Money Do You Want to Make?**
   Many people will take less money if a job is great in other ways–or to survive. Think about the minimum you would take as well as about what you would eventually like to earn. Your next job will probably be somewhere in between.

_____

_____

_____

_____

_____

7. **How Much Responsibility Are You Willing to Accept?**
   Usually, the jobs that pay the most require the greatest levels of responsibility. Do you want to work by yourself, be part of a group, or be in charge? If so, at what level?

_____

_____

_____

_____

_____

8. What Things Are Important to You?

Do you have values you want to include as a basis
of the work you do? For example, some people
want to help others, improve the environment,
build things, make machines work, gain power or
prestige, or care for animals or plants. Think about
what is important to you and how you might
include your values in your next job.

_____

_____

_____

_____

_____

Your Ideal Job

Is it possible to find a job that meets all the criteria you
have defined? Perhaps. Some people do–and the harder
you look, the more likely you are to find it. But, like most
people, you will probably have to compromise. So it's
useful to know in advance what things are *most* important
to you to have in your next job.

Don't be practical now. That can come later. Carefully
review the worksheet above and mark the things you
would most like to have in your ideal job. Narrow your list
to two or three criteria that are *the most important to you.*
Don't worry about a job title yet, or whether such a job
even exists.

Once you have identified your most important criteria, write them in the box below. You can simply list the items or write out a complete job objective. And, as always, you can add things that were not covered in the worksheet.

My Ideal Job Would Include ...

_____

_____

_____

_____

_____

_____

_____

Set a Specific Job Objective

You might find your ideal job in an occupational field you haven't yet considered. And, even if you are quite clear about the occupation, it's possible your ideal job is in an industry you're not familiar with. This combination of occupation and industry is the basis for your job search, and you should consider a variety of options.

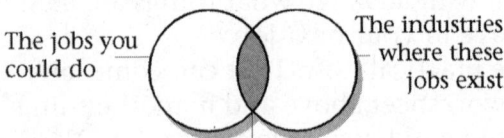

The jobs you could do

The industries where these jobs exist

Your ideal job exists in the overlap of those jobs that interest you most *and* in those industries that best meet your needs and interests!

The list below shows the 250 jobs in which about 85 percent of people in the United States work. A simple but effective way to explore job alternatives is to go through this list and check those that sound interesting. Then look up descriptions for the jobs you checked. The *Occupational Outlook Handbook* and *America's Top 300 Jobs* (both published by JIST) give thorough descriptions for all 250 jobs in the list. A good library will have one or the other of these books, and both are available from bookstores. I strongly encourage you to learn more about the jobs that interest you.

One of the best sources of industry information is the *Career Guide to America's Top Industries*. Also available in libraries and bookstores, this book reviews more than 40 major industries.

You will find these resources helpful in your job search. You can use the information in them to prepare for interviews, identify opportunities, and negotiate pay. Do use them. These and other sources of information are included in the bibliography at the back of this book.

The Top 250 Jobs in the U.S. Workforce

The jobs in this list are grouped in the same clusters as in the *Occupational Outlook Handbook* and *America's Top 300 Jobs,* and you can find full descriptions of them in those books.

The number to the right of each job refers to the percentage of employment change projected for that job through the year 2005. I obtained these projections from data provided by our friends at the U.S. Department of Labor. Most of the jobs have positive growth rates, although a few are negative. A 14-percent growth rate in overall employment is projected through 2005, so an occupation with a 14-percent growth rate would be "average."

I suggest you go through all the job groupings in the list and put a checkmark by those that seem interesting.

Then read about these jobs in the books cited above. Don't dismiss jobs with lower-than-average growth rates, because all occupations will have openings resulting from turnover, retirement, and other factors. And remember that these are national averages; your local situation could be much different.

Executive, Administrative, and Managerial Occupations	
Accountants and auditors	13
Administrative services managers	10
Budget analysts	12
Construction and building inspectors	22
Construction managers	28
Cost estimators	18
Education administrators	17
Employment interviewers	35
Engineering, science, and data processing managers	28
Financial managers	24
Funeral directors	11
General managers and top executives	15
Government chief executives and legislators	4
Health services managers	30
Hotel managers and assistants	26
Industrial production managers	-7
Inspectors and compliance officers, except construction	12
Loan officers and counselors	23
Management analysts and consultants	35
Marketing, advertising, and public relations managers	25
Personnel, training, and labor relations specialists and managers	22

Property and real estate managers	14
Purchasers and buyers	3
Restaurant and food service managers	33
Underwriters	7

Professional Specialty Occupations

Engineers	19
Aerospace engineers	6
Chemical engineers	13
Civil engineers	19
Electrical and electronics engineers	20
Industrial engineers	13
Mechanical engineers	19
Metallurgical, ceramic, and materials engineers	5
Mining engineers	-18
Nuclear engineers	4
Petroleum engineers	-21
Architects and surveyors	
Architects	17
Landscape architects	17
Surveyors	-3
Computer, mathematical, and operations research occupations	
Actuaries	4
Computer scientists and systems analysts	91
Mathematicians	5
Operations research analysts	50
Statisticians	3
Life scientists	

Agricultural scientists	19
Biological and medical scientists	127
Foresters and conservation scientists	18
Physical scientists	
Chemists	19
Geologists and geophysicists	17
Meteorologists	7
Physicists and astronomers	-9
Lawyers and judges	25
Social scientists and urban planners	23
Economists and marketing research analysts	25
Psychologists	23
Urban and regional planners	24
Social and recreation workers	
Human services workers	75
Recreation workers	20
Social workers	34
Clergy	
Protestant ministers	N/A
Rabbis	N/A
Roman Catholic priests	N/A
Teachers, librarians, and counselors	
Adult education teachers	28
Archivists and curators	19
College and university faculty	18
Counselors	31
Librarians	7

School teachers–Kindergarten, elementary, and secondary	22
Special education teachers	53
Health diagnosing occupations	
Chiropractors	29
Dentists	5
Optometrists	12
Physicians	22
Podiatrists	15
Veterinarians	11
Health assessment and treating occupations	
Dietitians and nutritionists	19
Occupational therapists	72
Pharmacists	17
Physical therapists	80
Physician assistants	23
Recreational therapists	22
Registered nurses	25
Respiratory therapists	36
Speech-language pathologists and audiologists	46
Communications occupations	
Public relations specialists	20
Radio and television announcers and newscasters	1
Reporters and correspondents	-4
Writers and editors	22
Visual arts occupations	
Designers	28

Photographers and camera operators	24
Visual artists	23
Performing arts occupations	
Actors, directors, and producers	30
Dancers and choreographers	24
Musicians	24

Technicians and Related Support Occupations

Health technologists and technicians	
Cardiovascular technologists and technicians	-5
Clinical laboratory technologists and technicians	12
Dental hygienists	42
Dispensing opticians	21
Electroneurodiagnostic technologists	28
Emergency medical technicians	36
Licensed practical nurses	28
Medical record technicians	56
Nuclear medicine technologists	26
Radiologic technologists	35
Surgical technicians	43
Technicians, except health	
Aircraft pilots	8
Air traffic controllers	N/A
Broadcast technicians	-4
Computer programmers	12
Drafters	N/A
Engineering technicians	9
Library technicians	21

Paralegals	58
Science technicians	13

Marketing and Sales Occupations

Cashiers	19
Counter and rental clerks	32
Insurance agents and brokers	4
Manufacturers' and wholesale sales representatives	10
Real estate agents, brokers, and appraisers	9
Retail sales worker supervisors and managers	17
Retail sales workers	14
Securities and financial services sales representatives	37
Services sales representatives	72
Travel agents	23

Administrative Support Occupations, Including Clerical

Adjusters, investigators, and collectors	22
Bank tellers	-27
Clerical supervisors and managers	19
Computer and peripheral equipment operators	-39
Credit clerks and authorizers	5
General office clerks	41
Information clerks	24
Hotel and motel desk clerks	20
Interviewing and new accounts clerks	20
Receptionists	31
Reservation and transportation ticket agents and travel clerks	-4

Mail clerks and messengers	-4
Material recording, scheduling, dispatching, and distributing workers	4
Dispatchers	15
Stock clerks	2
Traffic, shipping, and receiving clerks	4
Postal clerks and mail carriers	1
Record clerks	-8
Billing clerks and billing machine operators	-14
Bookkeeping, accounting, and auditing clerks	-8
Brokerage clerks and statement clerks	-9
File clerks	-15
Library assistants and bookmobile drivers	5
Order clerks	9
Payroll and timekeeping clerks	-9
Personnel clerks	-21
Secretaries	12
Stenographers, court reporters, and medical transcriptionists	-3
Teacher aides	39
Telephone operators	-16
Typists, word processors, and data entry keyers	-24

Service Occupations

Protective service occupations

Correctional officers	51
Firefighters	16
Guards	48
Police, detectives, and special agents	24

Private detectives and investigators	44
Food and beverage preparation and service occupations	
Chefs, cooks, and other kitchen workers	16
Food and beverage service workers	12
Health service occupations	
Dental assistants	42
Medical assistants	59
Nursing aides and psychiatric aides	29
Occupational therapy assistants and aides	82
Physical therapy assistants and aides	83
Personal and building service occupations	
Barbers and cosmetologists	15
Flight attendants	29
Homemaker-home health aides	107
Janitors and cleaners and cleaning supervisors	18
Preschool teachers and child-care workers	33
Private household workers	-16

Agriculture, Forestry, Fishing, and Related Occupations

Animal caretakers, except farm	26
Farm operators and managers	-21
Fishers, hunters, and trappers	-4
Forestry and logging workers	-5
Gardeners and groundskeepers	15

Mechanics, Installers, and Repairers

Aircraft mechanics and engine specialists	13
Automotive body repairers	17

Automotive mechanics	17
Diesel mechanics	17
Electronic equipment repairers	-9
Commercial and industrial electronic equipment repairers	2
Communications equipment mechanics	-35
Computer and office machine repairers	24
Electronic home entertainment equipment repairers	-10
Telephone installers and repairers	-70
Elevator installers and repairers	15
Farm equipment mechanics	14
General maintenance mechanics	18
Heating, air-conditioning, and refrigeration technicians	29
Home appliance and power tool repairers	-6
Industrial machinery repairers	8
Line installers and cable splicers	1
Millwrights	-15
Mobile heavy equipment mechanics	9
Motorcycle, boat, and small-engine mechanics	4
Musical instrument repairers and tuners	15
Vending machine servicers and repairers	-14

Construction Trades Occupations

Bricklayers and stonemasons	10
Carpenters	8
Carpet installers	9
Concrete masons and terrazzo workers	12
Drywall workers and lathers	7

Electricians	5
Glaziers	2
Insulation workers	20
Painters and paperhangers	16
Plasterers	11
Plumbers and pipefitters	4
Roofers	13
Sheetmetal workers	15
Structural and reinforcing ironworkers	5
Tilesetters	1

Production Occupations

Assemblers	
Precision assemblers	-3
Blue-collar worker supervisors	1
Food processing occupations	
Butchers and meat, poultry, and fish cutters	6
Inspectors, testers, and graders	**-4**
Metalworking and plastics-working occupations	
Boilermakers	-4
Jewelers	6
Machinists and tool programmers	-5
Metalworking and plastics-working machine operators	-6
Tool and die makers	-11
Welders, cutters, and welding machine operators	-3
Plant and systems operators	
Electric power generating plant operators and power distributors and dispatchers	-3

Stationary engineers	-10
Water and wastewater treatment plant operators	9
Printing occupations	
Bindery workers	6
Prepress workers	-10
Printing press operators	2
Textile, apparel, and furnishings occupations	
Apparel workers	-19
Shoe and leather workers and repairers	-28
Textile machinery operators	-13
Upholsterers	1
Woodworking occupations	2
Miscellaneous production occupations	
Dental laboratory technicians	-5
Ophthalmic laboratory technicians	12
Painting and coating machine operators	2
Photographic process workers	15

Transportation and Material Moving Occupations

Bus drivers	17
Material moving equipment operators	7
Rail transportation workers	-12
Taxi drivers and chauffeurs	22
Truck drivers	10
Water transportation workers	N/A

Handlers, Equipment Cleaners, Helpers, and Laborers	**10**
Job Opportunities in the Armed Forces	N/A

Chapter 3

Use Methods That Reduce Your Job Search Time

A recent survey found that 85 percent of all employers don't advertise job openings at all. They hire people they already know, people who find out about the jobs through word of mouth, or people who simply happen to be in the right place at the right time. Yes, sometimes this is a matter of luck, but there are ways to increase your "luck" in finding job openings.

Traditional Job Search Methods Are Not Very Effective

Most job seekers don't know how ineffective some traditional job hunting techniques are.

The chart that follows shows that fewer than 15 percent of all job seekers get jobs from reading want ads. Let's take a quick look at want ads and other traditional job search methods.

How People Find Jobs

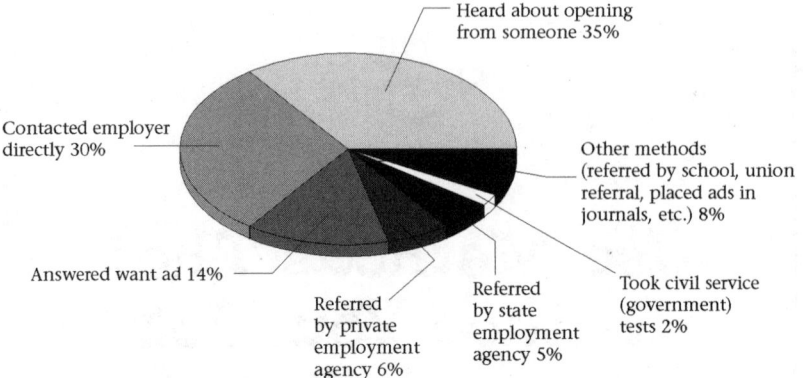

Heard about opening from someone 35%

Contacted employer directly 30%

Other methods (referred by school, union referral, placed ads in journals, etc.) 8%

Answered want ad 14%

Referred by private employment agency 6%

Referred by state employment agency 5%

Took civil service (government) tests 2%

QUIP

Whatever works is good. I am not suggesting you should never use less effective techniques. Some people get very good jobs using the worst methods, and that's fine with me. But I am suggesting you use a variety of methods and spend most of your time on the ones that work best for most people.

Help Wanted Ads. There's a good reason that only about 15 percent of all people get their jobs through the want ads: Everyone who reads the paper knows about those job openings, so competition for advertised jobs is fierce. Still, some people do get jobs this way, so go ahead and apply. Just be sure to spend *most* of your time on more effective methods.

The State Employment Service. Each state has a network of local offices that administer unemployment compensation and provide job leads and other services. These services are offered without charge to you or employers. Names vary by state, so the organization in your state may be called the Job Service, the Department of Labor, the Unemployment Office, or something else.

Nationally, only about 5 percent of all job seekers find their jobs through state employment services, and these organizations typically know only 10 percent (or less) of the actual job openings in a region. Still, it is worth a weekly visit. If you ask for the same counselor each week, you might impress the person enough so that he or she remembers you and refers you for the better openings.

You should also realize that some of the state employment services provide substantial help in the form of job search workshops and other resources. Look into it; the price is right–free!

Private Employment Agencies. Recent studies have found that private agencies work reasonably well for those who use them. But there are caveats to consider. First, these agencies typically work best for those seeking entry-level positions or those with specialized skills that are in demand. Most people who use a private agency end up finding their jobs from some other source.

Private agencies also charge a fee, either to you (often as high as 20 percent of your annual salary!) or to the employer. Most of them simply call employers asking if they have any openings, something you can do yourself. Unless you have skills that are in high demand, you may do better on your own–and save money. At the most, you should rely on a private agency as only *one* of the techniques you use and not depend on it too heavily.

Temporary Agencies. These can be sources of quick temporary jobs to bring in needed income and give you experience in a variety of settings–something that can help you land full-time jobs later. More and more employers are also using them to evaluate workers for permanent jobs. So consider using these agencies–especially if you need some income immediately–but be sure you continue an active search for a full-time job as well.

Sending Out Resumes. One survey found that most people would have to mail out more than 500 unsolicited resumes to get one interview! A much better approach is to simply call an employer to set up an interview directly, then send a resume. If you insist on sending out unsolicited resumes, do it on weekends. Save your "prime time" for more effective job search techniques.

Filling Out Applications. Most applications are used to *screen you out*. Larger organizations may require them, but remember this: *Your task is to get an interview, not fill out an application*. If you do complete one, make it neat, error-free, and do not include anything that could get you screened out. If necessary, leave a problematic section blank. You can always explain it after you get an interview.

Personnel Departments. Hardly anyone gets hired by interviewers in a personnel department. Their job is to screen you and refer the "best" applicants to the person who is actually hiring. You may need to cooperate with the folks in personnel, but it is often better to go directly to the person who is most likely to supervise you–even if no job opening exists at the moment. And remember that most organizations don't even have a personnel office, only the big ones!

The Two Job Search Methods That Work Best

It may surprise you but it's true: Two-thirds of all job seekers get their jobs using nontraditional methods. Often, these jobs are not advertised. They are part of the "hidden" job market. So how do you find them?

There are two basic nontraditional job search methods: (1) networking with people you know (warm contacts) and (2) making direct contacts with employers (cold contacts). Both are based on the most important job search rule of all.

▼

The Most Important Job Search Rule:

Don't wait until a job is open before contacting the employer!

Most jobs are filled by someone the employer meets before the job is formally "open." So the trick is to meet

*people who can hire you–before a job is available!
Instead of saying, "Do you have any jobs open?" say,
"I realize you may not have any openings now, but I
would still like to talk to you about the possibility of
future openings."*

Method 1: Develop a Network of Contacts in Five Easy Steps

One recent study found that 40 percent of all working people found their jobs through leads provided by a friend, a relative, or an acquaintance. That makes this method *the* most effective way to find a job. Developing new contacts is called *networking*. Here's how it works:

QUIP

Job seeking is a contact sport.
The old saying is true: You do have to know someone to get a job. I have found, though, that you can quickly get to know all sorts of new people, if you go about it in the right way. And often one of them will turn out to be the "someone" you need...

Step 1. Make lists of people you know. Make a list of everyone with whom you are friendly; then make a separate list of all your relatives. These two lists often add up to 25 to 100 people or more. Next, think of groups of people with whom you have something in common: for example, former co-workers or classmates; alumni from your high school or college; members of your social or sports groups; members of your professional association; former employers; and

members of your religious group. You may not know many of these people personally, but most will help you if you ask them.

Step 2. **Contact these people in a systematic way.** Each of these people is a contact for you. Obviously, some lists and some people on those lists will be more helpful than others, but almost any one of them could help you find a job lead.

Step 3. **Present yourself well.** Begin with your friends and relatives. Call and tell them you are looking for a job and need their help. Be as clear as possible about what you are looking for and what skills and qualifications you have. Read through the sample JIST Cards and phone script later in this chapter for presentation ideas.

Step 4. **Ask for leads.** It is possible that a friend or relative will know of a job opening just right for you. If so, get the details and get right on it! More likely, however, they will not, so here are three questions you should ask.

The Three Magic Networking Questions

1. *Do you know of any openings for a person with my skills? If the answer is "no" (which it usually is), then ask:*
2. *Do you know of someone else who might know of such an opening? If your contact does know someone, get that person's name and ask for another one. If he or she doesn't, ask:*
3. *Do you know someone who knows lots of people? If all else fails, this will usually get you a name.*

Step 5. Contact these referrals and ask them the same questions. For each original contact, you can extend your network by hundreds of people. Eventually, one of these people will hire you—or refer you to someone who will! This is networking, and it does work *if you are persistent.*

Method 2: Contact Employers Directly

It takes more courage, but contacting employers directly is a very effective job search technique. I call these cold contacts because you don't have an existing connection to the people you are calling. There are two basic techniques for making cold contacts: calling on the phone and dropping in without an appointment.

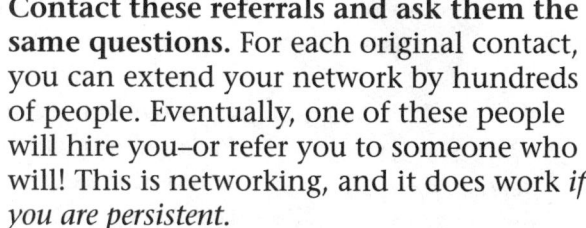

Three out of four jobs are never advertised because employers don't need to or want to advertise them. Employers trust people referred to them by someone they know far more than unknown strangers. Most jobs are filled in just this way, eliminating the need to advertise.

Use the "Yellow Pages"

The *Yellow Pages* is one of the best sources of potential employers available. You can easily use it as a source of cold contacts. Begin by looking at the index and asking for each entry, "Would an organization of this kind need a person with my skills?" If the answer is "yes," that type of organization or business becomes a possible target. You can also rate entries based on your interest, giving an A to those that look very interesting, a B to those you are unsure about, and a C to those that don't look interesting at all.

41

Next, select a type of organization that got a "yes" response (such as "hotels") and turn to that section of the *Yellow Pages*. Then call the businesses listed and ask to speak to the person who is most likely to hire or supervise someone with your skills. A sample telephone script is included later in this chapter.

Drop in Without an Appointment

You can also simply walk in to many potential employers' offices and ask to speak to the person in charge. This is particularly effective in small businesses, but it works surprisingly well in larger ones, too. Remember, you want an interview *even if there are no openings now.* If your timing is inconvenient, ask for a better time to come back for an interview.

Most Jobs Are with Small Employers

About 70 percent of all workers in the United States are employed by small businesses–those with 250 or fewer employees. While the largest corporations have reduced their numbers of employees in recent years, small businesses have been creating as many as 80 percent of all new jobs. There are often more opportunities to get training and promotions in smaller businesses, as well. Many do not even have personnel departments, so nontraditional job search techniques are particularly effective with them.

JIST Cards: Effective "Mini-Resumes"

JIST Cards are job search tools that get results. Typed, printed, or even neatly written on a 3-by-5-inch card, a JIST Card contains the essential information most employers want. Look at the sample cards below:

Sandy Zaremba

Home: (219) 232-7608   **Message:** (219) 234-7465

Position: General Office/Clerical

Over two years work experience plus one year of training in office practices. Type 55 wpm, trained in word processing operations, can post general ledger, handle payables, receivables, and most accounting tasks. Responsible for daily deposits averaging $10,000. Good interpersonal skills. Can meet strict deadlines and handle pressure well.

Willing to work any hours

Organized, honest, reliable, and hardworking

Chris Voorhees

Home: (602) 253-9678
Leave Message: (602) 257-6643

OBJECTIVE: Electronics—installation, maintenance, and sales

SKILLS: Four years work experience plus two years advanced training in electronics. A.S. degree in Electronics Engineering Technology. Managed a $300,000/yr. business while going to school full time, with grades in the top 25%. Familiar with all major electronic diagnostic and repair equipment. Hands-on experience with medical, consumer, communications, and industrial electronics equipment and applications. Good problem-solving and communication skills.

Customer service oriented.

Willing to do what it takes to get the job done.

JIST Cards are effective! Give them to friends and to each of your network contacts. Attach one to your resume. Enclose one in your thank-you note after an interview. Leave them with employers as "business cards." Use them in creative ways. They can be typed or even handwritten, but it is best to have 100 or more printed so you can put lots of them in circulation. Thousands of job seekers have used them because they get results!

QUIP

Dialing for dollars.
The phone is an essential job search tool. Using it effectively can get you more interviews per hour than any other job search tool I know of. But it won't work if you sit there waiting for people to call you. Use it heavily throughout your job search, and get an answering machine to take calls while you are out.

Use the Phone to Get Job Leads

Once you have created your JIST Card, it's easy to create a telephone contact script based on it. Adapt this basic script to call people you know or your *Yellow Pages* leads. Select *Yellow Pages* index categories that might have jobs for a person with your skills and get the numbers of specific businesses in those categories. Then ask for the person who is most likely to supervise you and present your phone script.

While it doesn't work every time, most people, with practice, can get one or more interviews in an hour by making these cold calls. Here is a phone script based on a JIST card:

"Hello, my name is Pam Nykanen. I'm interested in a position in hotel management. I have four years of experience in sales, catering, and

QUIP

Overcome phone phobia! Making cold calls takes courage, but it works. I've run programs in which job seekers routinely got two or more interviews in an hour using this technique. Start by calling people you know, and people they refer you to. Then try calls to businesses that don't sound very interesting. As you get better, call more desirable targets. Hey, what's the worst that can happen?

accounting with a 300-room hotel. I also have an associate degree in Hotel Management plus one year of experience with the Bradey Culinary Institute. During my employment, I helped double revenues from meetings and conferences and increased bar revenues by 46 percent. I have good problem-solving skills and am good with people. I'm also well-organized, hardworking, and detail-oriented. When can I come in for an interview?"

This example assumes you are calling someone you don't know, but the script can be modified easily to use with your warm contacts, including referrals.

Chapter 4

Redefine What "Counts" as an Interview, Then Get Two a Day

The average job seeker gets about five interviews per month–fewer than two a week. Yet many job seekers using the techniques presented here routinely get two interviews per day. Impossible, you say? Not at all. You just have to rewrite your definition of an interview.

The New Definition of an Interview

An interview is any face-to-face contact with someone who has the authority to hire or supervise a person with your skills–even if no opening exists at the time you interview.

With this definition, it is *much* easier to get interviews, because you can interview with all kinds of potential employers–not just those who have a job opening. Many job seekers in my workshops have used the *Yellow Pages* to get two interviews with just one hour of calls using the telephone contact script from Chapter 3. Others have simply dropped in on potential employers, asked for unscheduled interviews, *and gotten them.* And, of course, getting the names of other contacts from those you know–networking–is quite effective if you persist.

Getting two interviews a day means having 10 a week–and 40 a month. That's 800 percent more interviews than the average job seeker gets. Who do you think will get a job offer sooner? So set out each day to get at least two interviews. It *is* possible, once you know how.

Make Your Job Search a Full-Time Job

On average, job seekers spend fewer than 15 hours per week actually looking for work. The average length of unemployment ranges from three to four months, but some people take much longer (older workers and higher earners, for example). I believe there is a connection.

The simple truth is this: The more time you spend on your job search each week, the less time you are likely to remain unemployed. Of course, using more effective job search methods also helps. Those who use the nontraditional methods presented here have, again and again, gotten jobs in less than half the average time–and they often get better jobs too. Time management is the key, and the next section presents some tips to manage your job search time.

Spend at Least 25 Hours a Week Looking for a Job

If you are unemployed and looking for a full-time job, you should look on a full-time basis. It just makes sense to do so, although many do not. Many job seekers become nearly paralyzed by discouragement, lack of good techniques, and lack of structure. Most job seekers have no idea what they are going to be doing next Thursday–they don't have a plan. The most important beginning is to decide how many hours you can commit to your job search and stay with it. You should spend *a minimum of 25 hours a week* on hard-core job search activities. Let me walk you through a simple but effective process for organizing your job search schedule.

Write here how many hours you are willing to spend each week looking for a job: _____

Decide Which Days You Will Look for Work

Which days of the week will you spend looking for a job? _____

_____

How many hours will you look each day? _____
At what times will you begin and end your job search on each of these days? _____

_____

Create a Daily Schedule

Having a specific daily job search schedule is very important, because most job seekers find it hard to stay productive each day. You already know which job search methods are most effective, and you should plan to spend most of your time using those methods. The sample daily schedule that follows has been very effective for those who have used it, and it will give you ideas for your own. You are welcome to create your own schedule, of course, but I urge you to consider one similar to this. Why? Because it works.

A Daily Schedule That Works

7:00-8:00 A.M.	Get up, shower, dress, eat breakfast.
8:00-8:15 A.M.	Organize work space; review schedule for interviews or follow-ups; update schedule.
8:15-9:00 A.M.	Review old leads for follow-up; develop new leads (want ads, *Yellow Pages*, networking lists, etc.).
9:00-10:00 A.M.	Make phone calls, set up interviews.
10:00-10:15 A.M.	Take a break!
10:15-11:00 A.M.	Make more calls.
11:00-12:00 P.M.	Make follow-up calls as needed.

| 12:00-1:00 P.M. | Lunch break. |
| 1:00-5:00 P.M. | Go on interviews; call cold contacts in the field; research for upcoming interviews at the library. |

Do It Now! Get a Schedule Book and Write Down Your Schedule

This is important: If you are not accustomed to using a daily schedule book or planner, promise yourself you will get a good one tomorrow. Choose one that allows plenty of space for each day's plan on an hourly basis, plus room for daily "to do" lists. Write in your daily schedule in advance, then add interviews as they come. Get used to carrying your planner with you—and use it!

Chapter 5

Quick Tips That Make a Big Difference in the Interview

Interviews are where the job search action is. You have to get them, and you have to do well in them. If you've done your homework, you are now better able to get interviews for jobs that will best use your skills. This is very important, but your ability to effectively communicate your skills in the interview is what ultimately gets you the job.

It seems obvious that you should try to do well in interviews but, in fact, most people don't do well at all. For example, surveys of employers have found that as many as 80 percent of all applicants do not do a good job presenting the skills they have to do the jobs they say they want. Other surveys indicate that as many as 90 percent of all applicants do not provide adequate answers to problem questions.

An interview is a complex exchange, and I could write a book on that topic alone. (In fact, I have.) But there are a few simple things you can do to improve your interview performance enormously, and these are the things we will cover here.

The First Impression May Be the ONLY Impression You Make

If you make a negative first impression, you won't get a second chance to make a good one. Some research suggests that if the interviewer forms a negative impression in the first five minutes of the interview, your chances of getting a job offer are near zero. But I do not agree: I think you can screw things up much more quickly than that.

For example, a recent study found that interviewers rated 40 percent of all applicants as having dress or grooming problems that created a negative first impression. Forty percent! So, here is rule one for not getting eliminated too quickly:

Farr's Interview Dress and Grooming Rule

Dress and groom like the interviewer is likely to be dressed—but cleaner!

Dress for success! If necessary, get help selecting an interview outfit from someone who dresses well. Pay close attention to your grooming, too. Little things count.

Quick Tips for Creating a Good Impression

- ☼ **Be early:** Be about five minutes early for every interview.
- ☼ **Treat the receptionist with respect:** Assume that anything you say will be reported to the interviewer. Treating a receptionist badly is often a quick way to get screened out.
- ☼ **Make all correspondence neat and error-free:** Be sure your resume, letters, thank-you notes, and other correspondence are neat and error-free. This creates an impression too.
- ☼ **Make small talk:** The first few minutes of an interview are often informal. This is when the interviewer can judge your ability to socialize. This is a good time to comment positively on something you notice in the interviewer's office. My brother once commented enthusiastically on a painting in an interviewer's office. It turned out that the interviewer was the painter, and my brother got the offer.
- ☼ **Do your homework:** Read up on the job you are applying for and the industry before you go in. And find out something about the organization *before you go in.*

A Traditional Interview Is Not a Friendly Exchange

Before we get to techniques for answering questions, it's important to understand what is going on. In a traditional interview situation, there is a job opening and you are one of several applicants for the job. In this setting, the employer's task is to eliminate all but one applicant.

55

Assuming that you've gotten as far as an interview, the interviewer's questions are designed to elicit information that can be used to screen you out. If you are wise, you know that your task is to avoid getting screened out. It's not an open and honest interaction, is it?

This illustrates yet another advantage of nontraditional job search techniques: the opportunity to talk to an employer before an opening exists. This eliminates the stress of a traditional interview. Employers are not trying to screen you out, and you are not trying to keep them from finding out stuff about you.

Having said that, knowing how to answer questions that might be asked in a traditional interview is good preparation for whatever you might run into during your job search.

How to Answer Tough Interview Questions

Your answers to a few key problem questions often determine whether you get a job offer or not. While there are thousands of problem questions you might be asked, I have listed just ten below. If you can answer these well, you are prepared for most interviews.

▼

The Top 10 Problem Questions

1. Why don't you tell me about yourself?
2. Why should I hire you?
3. What are your major strengths?
4. What are your major weaknesses?
5. What sort of pay do you expect to receive?
6. How does your previous experience relate to the jobs we have here?
7. What are your plans for the future?
8. What will your former employer (or references) say about you?
9. Why are you looking for this type of position, and why here?
10. Why don't you tell me about your personal situation?

I don't have the space here to give complete answers to all of these questions, and there are potentially hundreds more. Instead, let me suggest several techniques that you can use to answer almost any interview question.

The Three-Step Process for Answering Questions

I know this might seem too simple, but the Three-Step Process is easy to remember and allows you to evaluate a question and devise a good answer. The technique is based on sound principles and has worked for thousands of people, so consider trying it.

▼

The three steps are:

1. **Understand what is really being asked.**
2. **Answer the question briefly.**
3. **Answer the real concern.**

Let's review each of these steps.

 Step 1. Understand What Is Really Being Asked

Most questions are designed to find out about your self-management skills and personality. While they are rarely this blunt, the employer's *real* question is often:

- ☼ Can I depend on you?
- ☼ Are you easy to get along with?
- ☼ Are you a good worker?
- ☼ Do you have the experience and training to do the job?
- ☼ Are you likely to stay on the job for a reasonable period of time and be productive?

Ultimately, if the employer is not convinced you will stay and be a good worker, it won't matter if you have the best credentials—he or she won't hire you.

Step 2. Answer the Question Briefly

- ☼ Acknowledge the facts, but . . .
- ☼ Present them as an advantage, not a disadvantage.

There are many interview questions that encourage you to provide negative information. The classic is, "What are your major weaknesses?" Obviously, this is a trick question, and many people are just not prepared for it. A good response is to mention something that is not very damaging, such as, "I've been told I am a perfectionist, sometimes not delegating as effectively as I might." But your answer is not complete until you continue with Step 3.

Step 3. Answer the Real Concern by Presenting Your Related Skills

☼ Base your answer on the key skills you have. Give examples to support your skills statements.

For example, an employer might say to a recent graduate, "We were looking for someone with more experience in this field. Why should we consider you?"

Here is one possible answer:

"I'm sure there are people who have more experience, but I do have more than six years of work experience, including three years of advanced training and hands-on experience using the latest methods and

techniques. And because my training is recent, I am open to new ideas and am used to working hard and learning quickly."

In the example from Step 2 (about your need to delegate), a good skills statement might be, "I have been working on this problem and have learned to allow my staff to do things, making sure they have good training and supervision. I've found that their performance improves, and it frees me up to do other things."

Whatever your situation, learn to use it to your advantage. It's essential to communicate your skills during an interview, and The Three-Step Process lets you answer problem questions while showcasing those skills. It works!

Salary Negotiations—A Few Techniques to Help You Earn Thousands of Dollars a Minute

Here are a few essential things to remember when it comes time to negotiate your pay.

> ### The only time to negotiate is after you have been offered the job.

Early in the screening process, employers what to know how much money you want so they can eliminate you from consideration. They figure if you want too much, you won't be happy with the job and won't stay. And if you will take too little, they might think you don't have enough experience. So *never* discuss your salary expectations until you are offered the job.

> ### If pressed, speak in terms of a wide pay range.

If you are pushed to reveal your pay expectations early in an interview, ask the interviewer what the company's normal pay range is for the job. He or she will often tell you, and you can say that you would consider an offer in this range. If you are forced to be more specific, speak in terms of a wide range. For example, if you figure they are likely to pay from $20,000 to $25,000, say that you would consider any fair offer in the low to mid-20s. This statement covers their range *and goes a bit higher*. If all else fails, tell them that you would consider any reasonable offer.

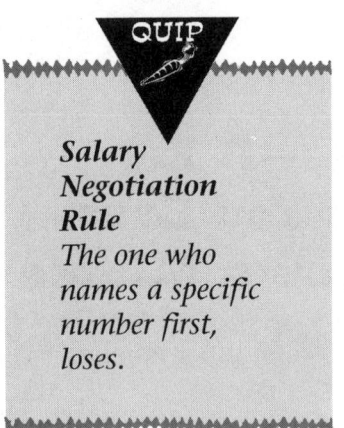

Salary Negotiation Rule
The one who names a specific number first, loses.

You need to know, in advance, what the job is likely to pay so that you are prepared for this line of questioning. A variety of books provide this information, or you can simply ask people who do similar work for the pay ranges for this type of job.

Don't say "no" too quickly.

Never, *never* turn down a job offer during an interview! Even if you are shocked at how little the job pays, thank the interviewer and ask to consider the offer overnight. You can turn it down tomorrow, telling the interviewer how much you appreciate the offer and asking him or her to consider you for other jobs that pay better or whatever. This is no time to be playing games: If you want the job, you should say so. And it's okay to ask for additional pay or other concessions. But if you simply can't accept the offer, say why and ask to be kept in mind for future opportunities. You just never know.

Close the Interview Effectively

Most interviews simply end with a fizzle, but there are some things you can do as an interview is winding up that can make a difference. Even if you are not certain you want the job, it is wise to go after a job offer–you can always turn it down later.

- ☼ **Emphasize your key skills.** Tell the interviewer why he or she should hire you over someone else. Review the skills you have to do this job.
- ☼ **Ask for the job.** If you want the job, say so. Employers want to hire people who are enthusiastic about the work.
- ☼ **Arrange to call back.** Ask for a specific time and date to call the employer back and ask questions or learn of your status.

Remember, the interview is where the hiring decision is made. Concentrate on making a good impression and emphasizing your skills.

Chapter 6

Follow Up on All Contacts

It's a fact: People who follow up with potential employers and with others in their network get jobs faster than those who do not. So I've put together a few simple rules to guide you throughout your job search. Use them, they work.

Four Rules for Effective Follow-Up

1. *Send a thank-you note to each person who helps you in your job search.*
2. *Send the thank-you note within 24 hours after speaking with the person.*
3. *Enclose JIST Cards with your thank-you notes and all other correspondence.*
4. *Develop a system to keep following up with good contacts.*

Thank-You Notes Make a Difference

Thank-you notes can be handwritten or typed on quality paper with matching envelopes. Keep them simple, neat, and error-free. Following is a sample:

April 16, 19XX

2234 Riverwood Ave.
Philadelphia, PA 17963

Ms. Sandra Kijek
Henderson & Associates, Inc.
1801 Washington Blvd., Suite 1201
Philadelphia, PA 17963

Dear Ms. Kijek:

Thank you for sharing your time with me so generously today. I really appreciated seeing your state-of-the-art computer equipment.

Your advice has already proved helpful. I have an appointment to meet with Mr. Robert Hopper on Friday as you anticipated.

Please consider referring me to others if you think of someone else who might need a person with my skills.

Sincerely,

William Richardson

William Richardson

QUIP

Use Job Lead Cards to Organize Your Contacts

High-tech help.
Good contact management software can also help you organize your follow-up activities. But many people find that the simple card file system works very well, and they use their computers for word processing tasks.

Use simple 3-by-5-inch cards to keep essential information on every person in your network. Buy a card file box with tabs for each day of the month. File the cards under the date you want to contact the person, and the rest is easy. I've found that staying in touch with a good contact every other week can pay off big. Here's a sample card to give you ideas for creating your own:

ORGANIZATION: _Mutual Health Insurance_

CONTACT PERSON: _Anna Tomey_   PHONE: _317-355-0216_

SOURCE OF LEAD: _Aunt Ruth_

NOTES: _4/10 Called. Anna on vacation. Call back 4/15. 4/15 Interview set 4/20 at 1:30. 4/20 Anna showed me around. They use the same computers we used in school! (Friendly people) Sent thank-you note and JIST Card, call back 5/1. 5/1 Second interview 5/8 at 9_

Chapter 7

Resumes: Write a Simple One Now and a Better One Later

You've already learned that sending out resumes and waiting for responses is not an effective job seeking technique. However, many employers will ask you for them, and they are useful tools in your job search. I suggest that you begin with a simple resume that you can complete quickly. I've seen too many people spend weeks working on their resumes when they could have been out getting interviews instead. If you want a "better" resume, you can work on it on weekends and evenings. So let's begin with the basics.

Tips for Creating a Superior Resume

One problem with resumes is that everyone is an "expert." If you ask ten people for advice on your resume, you'll probably get ten different ideas about what you should change. So don't worry about it too much. You're better off using a simple but acceptable resume than spending hours working on a "better" one.

The following tips make sense for any resume format.

☼ **Write it yourself.** It's okay to look at other resumes for ideas, but write your own yourself. It will force you to organize your thoughts and background.

☼ **Make it error-free.** One spelling or grammar error will create a negative impressionist. (See what I mean?) Get someone else to review your final draft for any errors. Then review it again, because these rascals have a way of slipping in.

☼ **Make it look good.** Poor copy quality, cheap paper, bad type quality, or anything else that creates a poor appearance will turn off employers to even the best resume content. Get professional help with design and printing if necessary. Many resume writers and print shops have desktop publishing services and can do design for you.

☼ **Be brief, be relevant.** Many good resumes fit on one page, and few justify more than two. Include only the most important points. Use short sentences and action words. If it doesn't relate to and support the job objective, cut it!

☼ **Be honest.** Don't overstate your qualifications. If you end up getting a job you can't handle, it will not be to your advantage. Most employers will see right through a lie anyway.

Many resume experts suggest that creating a "dynamite" or "perfect" resume will make yours jump out of the pile. This is old-fashioned advice. It assumes you are applying to large personnel offices and for advertised jobs when, in today's job market, most jobs are not advertised and are with small employers. My advice is to avoid getting into that stack of resumes in the first place by looking for openings that others overlook.

☼ **Be positive.** Emphasize your accomplishments and results. This is no place to be humble or to display your faults.

☼ **Be specific.** Rather than saying, "I am good with people," say, "I supervised four people in the warehouse and increased productivity by 30 percent." Use numbers whenever possible, such as the number of people served, percentage sales increase, or dollars saved.

You should also know that everyone feels he or she is a resume expert. Whatever you do, someone will tell you it is wrong. It's important to understand that a resume is a job search tool. You should never delay or slow down your job search because your resume is not "good enough." The best approach is to create a simple and acceptable resume as quickly as possible, then use it. As time permits, create a better one if you feel you must.

Chronological Resumes

Most resumes use the chronological format. It is a simple format in which the most recent experience is listed first, followed by each previous job. This arrangement works fine for someone with work experience in several similar jobs, but not as well for those with limited experience or for career changers.

Look at the two resumes for Judith Jones that follow. Both use the chronological approach, but the second one includes some improvements over the first. The improved resume is clearly better, but either would be acceptable to most employers.

Tips for Writing a Simple Chronological Resume

Here are some tips for writing a basic chronological resume.

- ☼ **Name.** Use your formal name rather than a nickname if it sounds more professional.
- ☼ **Address.** Be complete. Include your zip code and avoid abbreviations. If moving is a possibility, use the address of a friend or relative or be certain to include a forwarding address.
- ☼ **Telephone Number.** Employers are most likely to try to reach you by phone, so including a reliable way you can be reached is very important. Always include your area code, because you never know where your resume might travel. If you don't have an answering machine, get one–and make sure you leave it on whenever you are not home. Listen to your message to be sure it presents you in a professional way. A variety of communication systems are also available: for example, voice mail, professional answering services, beepers, mobile phones, and on-line e-mail programs. If you provide an alternative phone number or another way to reach you, make it clear to the caller what to expect.

70

Sample of a simple chronological resume.

Judith J. Jones

115 South Hawthorne Avenue
Chicago, Illinois 46204
(312) 653-9217 (home)
(312) 272-7608 (message)

JOB OBJECTIVE

Desire a position in the office management, secretarial, or clerical area. Prefer a position requiring responsibility and a variety of tasks.

EDUCATION AND TRAINING

Acme Business College, Chicago, Illinois
Graduate of a one-year business/secretarial program, 1996

John Adams High School, South Bend, Indiana
Diploma: Business Education

U.S. Army

Financial procedures, accounting functions. Other: Continuing education classes and workshops in Business Communication, Scheduling Systems, and Customer Relations.

EXPERIENCE

1995-1997 — Returned to school to complete and update my business skills. Learned word processing and other new office techniques.

1992-1995 — Claims Processor, Blue Spear Insurance Co., Chicago, Illinois. Handled customer medical claims, filed, miscellaneous clerical duties.

1990-1992 — Sales Clerk, Judy's Boutique, Chicago, Illinois. Responsible for counter sales, display design, and selected tasks.

1988-1990 — Specialist, U.S. Army. Assigned to various stations as a specialist in finance operations. Promoted prior to honorable discharge.

Previous Jobs — Held part-time and summer jobs throughout high school.

PERSONAL

I am reliable, hardworking, and good with people.

Judith J. Jones

115 South Hawthorne Avenue
Chicago, Illinois 46204
(312) 653-9217 (home)
(312) 272-7608 (message)

JOB OBJECTIVE

Seeking position requiring excellent management and secretarial skills in an office environment. Position should require a variety of tasks including typing, word processing, accounting/bookkeeping functions, and customer contact.

EDUCATION AND TRAINING

Acme Business College, Chicago, Illinois.
Completed one-year program in Professional Secretarial and Office Management. Grades in top 30 percent of my class. Courses: word processing, accounting theory and systems, time management, basic supervision, and others.

John Adams High School, South Bend, Indiana.
Graduated with emphasis on business and secretarial courses. Won shorthand contest.

Other: Continuing education at my own expense (Business Communications, Customer Relations, Computer Applications, other courses).

EXPERIENCE

1995-1997 — Returned to business school to update skills. Advanced course work in accounting and office management. Learned to operate word processing and PC-based accounting and spreadsheet software. Gained operating knowledge of computers.

1992-1995 — Claims Processor, Blue Spear Insurance Company, Chicago, Illinois. Handled 50 complex medical insurance claims per day — 18 percent above department average. Received two merit raises for performance.

1990-1992 — Assistant Manager, Judy's Boutique, Chicago, Illinois. Managed sales, financial records, inventory, purchasing, correspondence, and related tasks during owner's absence. Supervised four employees. Sales increased 15 percent during my tenure.

1988-1990 — Finance Specialist (E4), U.S. Army. Responsible for the systematic processing of 500 invoices per day from commercial vendors. Trained and supervised eight employees. Devised internal system allowing 15 percent increase in invoices processed with a decrease in personnel.

1984-1988 — Various part-time and summer jobs through high school. Learned to deal with customers, meet deadlines, work hard, and other skills.

SPECIAL SKILLS AND ABILITIES

Type 80 words per minute and can operate most office equipment. Good communication and math skills. Accept supervision, able to supervise others. Excellent attendance record.

- ☼ **Job Objective.** This is optional for a basic resume, but it is important to include. Notice that Judy is keeping her options open with her objective. Writing "Secretary" or "Clerical" might limit her to lower-paying jobs or prevent her from being considered for other jobs she might take.
- ☼ **Education and Training.** Include any formal training you've had plus any training that supports the job you are seeking. If you did not finish a formal degree or program, list what you did complete. Include any special accomplishments.
- ☼ **Previous Experience.** The standard approach is to list your employer, the job title you held, the dates you were employed, and your responsibilities. But there are better ways of presenting your experience. Look over the "Improved Chronological Resume" for ideas. The improved version emphasizes results, accomplishments, and performance.
- ☼ **Personal Data.** Neither of the samples includes the standard height, weight, or marital status listed on so many resumes. This information is simply not relevant! If you do include personal information, put it at the bottom and keep it related to the job you want.
- ☼ **References.** There is no need to list references. If employers want them, they will ask. If your references are particularly good, it's okay to say so.

Tips for an Improved Chronological Resume

Once you have a simple, error-free, and eye-pleasing resume, get on with your job search. There is no reason to delay! But if you want to create a better one in your spare time (evenings or weekends), here are some additional tips.

- ☼ **Job Objective.** A poorly written job objective can limit the type of jobs for which you will be considered. Think of the kind of work you want to do and can do well, and describe it in general terms. Instead of writing "Restaurant Manager," write "Manage a small to mid-sized business," if that is what you are qualified to do.

- ☼ **Education and Training.** New graduates should emphasize their recent training and education more than those with five or more years of recent and related work experience. Think about any special accomplishments you achieved while in school and include them if they relate to the job. Did you work full-time while in school? Did you do particularly well in work-related classes, get an award, or participate in sports?

- ☼ **Skills and Accomplishments.** Employers are interested in what you accomplished and did well. Include things that relate to doing well in the job you are seeking now. Even "small" things count. Maybe your attendance was perfect, you met a tight deadline, or did the work of others during vacations. Be specific, and include numbers–even if you have to estimate them.
- ☼ **Job Titles.** Many job titles don't accurately reflect the job you did. For example, your job title may have been "Cashier" but you also opened the store, trained new staff, and covered for the boss on vacations. Perhaps "Head Cashier and Assistant Manager" would be more accurate. Check with your previous employer if you are not sure.
- ☼ **Promotions.** If you were promoted or got good evaluations, say so. A promotion to a more responsible job can be handled as a separate job, if this makes sense.
- ☼ **Problem Areas.** Employers look for any sign of instability or lack of reliability. It is very expensive to hire and train someone who won't stay or who won't work out. Gaps in employment, jobs held for short periods of time, or a lack of direction in the jobs

you've held are all red flags for employers. If you
have any legitimate explanation, use it. For example:

"1994 ~ Continued my education at . . ."

"1995 ~ Traveled extensively throughout the
United States."

"1995 to present ~ Self-employed barn painter
and widget maker."

"1996 ~ Had first child, took year off before
returning to work."

Use entire years or even seasons of years to avoid
displaying a shorter gap you can't explain easily: "Spring
1994 ~ Fall 1995" will not show you as unemployed from
October to November 1995, for example.

Skills and Combination Resumes

QUIP

*Resumes are
not effective
tools for
getting
interviews.
A better
approach is to
make direct
contact with
those who hire or
supervise people
with your skills
(even if there are
no openings
available) and
ask for an
interview. Then
send a resume.*

The functional or "skills"
resume emphasizes your most
important skills, supported by
specific examples of how you
have used them. This approach
allows you to use any part of your
life history to support your ability
to do the job you are seeking.

While a skills resume can be
very effective, it does require
more work to create one. And
some employers don't like them
because they can hide a job
seeker's faults (such as job gaps,
lack of formal education, or
deficit of related work
experience) better than a
chronological resume.

Still, a skills resume may
make sense for you. Look over
the sample resumes that follow
for ideas. Notice that one
resume includes elements of a

skills and a chronological resume. This is called a "combination" resume–an approach that makes sense if your previous job history or education and training is positive.

Sample of a simple skills resume.

ALAN ATWOOD

3231 East Harbor Road

Woodland Hills, California 91367

Home: (818) 447-2111   Message (818) 547-8201

Objective: A responsible position in retail sales

Areas of Accomplishment:

Customer Service
- Communicate well with all age groups.
- Able to interpret customer concerns to help them find the items they want.
- Received 6 Employee of the Month awards in 3 years.

Merchandise Display
- Developed display skills via in-house training and experience.
- Received Outstanding Trainee Award for Christmas toy display.
- Dress mannequins, arrange table displays, and organize sale merchandise.

Stock Control and Marketing
- Maintained and marked stock during department manager's 6-week illness.
- Developed more efficient record-keeping procedures.

Additional Skills
- Operate cash register, IBM compatible hardware, calculators, and electronic typewriters.
- Punctual, honest, reliable, and a hard-working self-starter.

Experience:
Harper's Department Store
Woodland Hills, California
1995 to Present

Education:
Central High School
Woodland Hills, California
3.6/4.0 Grade Point Average
Honor Graduate in Distributive Education
Two years retail sales training in
Distributive Education. Also courses in Business
Writing, Accounting, Typing, and Word Processing.

> *Sample skills resume for someone with substantial experience—but using only one page. Note that no dates are included.*

Ann McLaughlin

Career Objective	Challenging position in programming or related areas which would best utilize expertise in the business environment. This position should have many opportunities for an aggressive, dedicated individual with leadership abilities to advance.
Programming Skills	Include functional program design relating to business issues including payroll, inventory and database management, sales, marketing, accounting, and loan amortization reports. In conjunction with design would be coding, implementation, debugging, and file maintenance. Familiar with distributed network systems including PC's and Mac's and working knowledge of DOS, UNIX, COBOL, BASIC, RPG, and FORTRAN. Also familiar with mainframe environments including DEC, Prime, and IBM, including tape and disk file access, organization, and maintenance.
Areas of Expertise	Interpersonal communication strengths, public relations capabilities, innovative problem-solving and analytical talents.
Sales	A total of nine years experience in sales and sales management. Sold security products to distributors and burglar alarm dealers. Increased company's sales from $16,000 to over $70,000 per month. Creatively organized sales programs and marketing concepts. Trained sales personnel in prospecting techniques while also training service personnel in proper installation of burglar alarms. Result: 90% of all new business was generated through referrals from existing customers.
Management	Managed burglar alarm company for four years while increasing profits yearly. Supervised office, sales, and installation personnel. Supervised and delegated work to assistants in accounting functions and inventory control. Worked as assistant credit manager, responsible for over $2 million per month in sales. Handled semiannual inventory of five branch stores totaling millions of dollars and supervised 120 people.
Accounting	Balanced all books and prepared tax forms for burglar alarm company. Eight years experience in credit and collections, with emphasis on collections. Collection rates were over 98% each year, and was able to collect a bad debt in excess of $250,000 deemed "uncollectible" by company.
Education	School of Computer Technology, Pittsburgh, PA Business Applications Programming/TECH EXEC- 3.97 GPA Robert Morris College, Pittsburgh, PA Associate degree in Accounting, Minor in Management

2306 Cincinnati Street, Kingsford, PA 15171 (412) 437-6217
Message: (412) 464-1273

THOMAS P. MARRIN

80 Harrison Avenue ● Baldwin L.I., New York 11563 ● Answering Service: (716) 223-4705

OBJECTIVE:
A middle/upper-level management position with responsibilities including problem solving, planning, organizing, and budget management.

EDUCATION:
University of Notre Dame, B.S. in Business Administration. Course emphasis on accounting, supervision, and marketing. Upper 25% of class. Additional training: Advanced training in time management, organization behavior, and cost control.

MILITARY:
U.S. Army — 2nd Infantry Division, 1985 to 1989, 1st Lieutenant and platoon leader — stationed in Korea and Ft. Knox, Kentucky. Supervised an annual budget of nearly $4 million and equipment valued at over $40 million. Responsible for training, scheduling, and activities of as many as 40 people. Received several commendations. Honorable discharge.

BUSINESS EXPERIENCE:
Wills Express Transit Co., Inc. — Mineola, New York

Promoted to Vice President, Corporate Equipment — 1994 to Present
Controlled purchase, maintenance, and disposal of 1100 trailers and 65 company cars with $6.7 million operating and $8.0 million capital expense responsibilities.
• Scheduled trailer purchases, six divisions.
• Operated 2.3% under planned maintenance budget in company's second best profit year while operating revenues declined 2.5%.
• Originated schedule to correlate drivers' needs with available trailers.
• Developed systematic Purchase and Disposal Plan for company car fleet.
• Restructured Company Car Policy, saving 15% on per car cost.

Promoted to Asst. Vice President, Corporate Operations — 1993 to 1994
Coordinated activities of six sections of Corporate Operations with an operating budget over $10 million.
• Directed implementation of zero-base budgeting.
• Developed and prepared Executive Officer Analyses detailing achievable cost reduction measures. Resulted in cost reduction of over $600,000 in first two years.
• Designed policy and procedure for special equipment leasing program during peak seasons. Cut capital purchases by over $1 million.

Manager of Communications — 1991 to 1993
Directed and managed $1.4 million communication network involving 650 phones, 150 WATS lines, 3 switchboards, 1 teletype machine, 5 employees.
• Installed computerized WATS Control System. Optimized utilization of WATS lines and pinpointed personal abuse. Achieved payback earlier than originally projected.
• Devised procedures that allowed simultaneous 20% increase in WATS calls and a $75,000/year savings.

Hayfield Publishing Company, Hempstead, New York

Communications Administrator — 1989 to 1991
Managed daily operations of a large Communications Center. Reduced costs and improved services.

Even more resumes: I've included more sample resumes in Appendix B. Look them over for ideas and inspiration in writing your own.

The Quick Job Search Review

This winds up the content on career planning and job seeking for this book. Yes, I know it was short–I intentionally kept it as short as I could while still presenting the essential techniques for effective career planning and job seeking. There is a lot more detail in my other books, should you want it, but this is enough to get you started–and may be all you need to know to get a better job in less time. I hope this will be true for you, and I wish you well in your search.

The rest of the book provides information you might find of interest. But before you go any further, let's review the most important points on the topic of job seeking:

1. Approach your job search as if it were a job itself.
2. Get organized, and spend at least 25 hours per week actively looking.
3. Follow up on all the leads you generate, and send out lots of thank-you notes and JIST Cards.
4. If you want to get a good job quickly, work on getting lots of interviews!
5. Pay attention to the details, then be yourself in the interview. Remember that employers are people too. They will hire someone they feel will do the job well, be reliable, and fit easily into the work environment.
6. When you want the job, tell the employer that you want the job and why. You need to have a good answer to the question, "Why should I hire you?" It's that simple.

Few people will get a job offer because someone knocks on their door and offers one. The craft of job seeking involves some luck, but you are far more likely to get lucky if you are out getting interviews. Structure your job search as if it were a full-time job, and try not to get discouraged. There are lots of jobs out there, and someone needs what you can do. Your job is to find them.

I hope this little book helps, though you should consider learning more. Career planning and job seeking skills are adult survival skills for our new economy. Good luck!

Mike Farr

79

A·p·p·e·n·d·i·x A

Essential Job Search Data Worksheet

Completing the worksheet that follows will help you create your resume, fill out applications, and answer interview questions. Take it with you as a reference when you're looking for a job. Use an erasable pen or pencil so you can make changes. In all sections, emphasize the skills and accomplishments that best support your ability to do the job you want. Use extra sheets as needed!

Key Accomplishments

List three accomplishments that best prove your ability to do well in the kind of job you want.

1. _____

_____

2. _____

_____

3. _____

_____

Education/Training

Name of high school(s)/years attended: _____

_____

_____

_____

_____

_____

Subjects related to job objective: _____

_____

_____

_____

_____

_____

Extracurricular activities/Hobbies/Leisure activities:

_____

_____

_____

_____

_____

Accomplishments/Things you did well: _____

_____

_____

_____

_____

_____

Schools you attended after high school, years attended, degrees/certificates earned: _____

_____

_____

_____

_____

_____

Courses related to job objective: _____

_____

_____

_____

_____

_____

Extracurricular activities/Hobbies/Leisure activities:

_____

_____

_____

_____

_____

Accomplishments/Things you did well: _____

_____

_____

_____

_____

Military, on-the-job, or informal training, such as from a hobby; dates of training; type of certificate earned: _____

_____

_____

_____

_____

Specific things you can do as a result: _____

_____

_____

_____

_____

Work and Volunteer History

List your most recent job first, followed by each previous job. Include military experience and unpaid work here, too, if it makes sense to do so. Use additional sheets to cover *all* your significant jobs or unpaid experiences.

Whenever possible, provide numbers to support what you did: number of people served over one or more years, number of transactions processed, percentage sales increase, total inventory value you were responsible for, payroll of the staff you supervised, total budget you were responsible for. As much as possible, mention results using numbers–they can be impressive when mentioned in an interview or on a resume.

Job #1 _____

Name of organization: _____

_____

_____

Address: _____

_____

_____

Phone number: _____

Dates employed: _____

Job title(s): _____

_____

_____

Supervisor's name: _____

_____

Details of any raises or promotions: _____

_____

_____

Machinery or equipment you handled: _____

_____

_____

Special skills this job required: _____

_____

_____

List what you accomplished or did well: _____

_____

_____

Job #2 _____
Name of organization: _____

_____

_____

Address: _____

_____

_____

Phone number: _____
Dates employed: _____
Job title(s): _____

_____

_____

Supervisor's name: _____

_____

_____

Details of any raises or promotions: _____

_____

_____

Machinery or equipment you handled: _____

_____

_____

Special skills this job required: _____

_____

_____

List what you accomplished or did well: _____

_____

_____

Job #3 _____

Name of organization: _____

_____

_____

Address: _____

_____

_____

Phone number: _____

Dates employed: _____

Job title(s): _____

_____

_____

Supervisor's name: _____

_____

_____

Details of any raises or promotions: _____

_____

_____

Machinery or equipment you handled: _____

_____

_____

Special skills this job required: _____

_____

_____

List what you accomplished or did well: _____

_____

_____

References

Contact your references and let them know what type of job you want and why you are qualified. Be sure to review what they will say about you. Because some employers will not give out references by phone or in person, have previous employers write a

letter of reference for you in advance. If you are worried about a bad reference from a previous employer, negotiate what they will say about you or get written references from other people you worked with. When creating your list, be sure to include each reference's name and job title, where he or she works, a business address and phone number, how that person knows you, and what that person will say about you.

Appendix B

More Sample Resumes

As I've said before, sending out unsolicited resumes is *not* an effective technique for getting interviews.

There are several reasons people persist in thinking that resumes will work for them. First, it's nice to think that sending in a piece of paper will get you an interview. Sending out resumes is *a lot* less threatening to most people than calling up a stranger and risking direct rejection. A second reason is that so many "experts" suggest that creating a better/best/perfect/dynamite resume will get you a job because your better/best/perfect/dynamite resume will just jump out of the pile and get you an interview.

These resume experts are singing an old-fashioned tune. Their underlying assumption is that your job search will consist of looking for advertised openings, which get lots of resumes in response–or that your resume will end up in a personnel department. But you now know that three out of four jobs are not advertised. And you know that about 70 percent of all jobs are now with smaller employers, who usually don't even have personnel offices. And, even if you *do* want to work in a larger organization, you know that your objective is to get to the person who is most likely to hire or supervise someone with your skills–and that person is unlikely to work in personnel.

Having said all this, I still believe a good resume is important for most job seekers. Employers will ask for them, so you should have one. And the *process of writing* a good resume will help you clarify the skills, accomplishments, and experiences that best support your ability to do the job you want.

Writing a good resume takes time, but time spent on worrying about your resume will *not* help you get interviews. So my advice on resume writing is quite simple:

1. Write a simple and error-free resume today, and use it in your job search tomorrow.

2. If you want a better resume, work on one at night and weekends. Save your weekdays for getting interviews.

3. The best way to get interviews is to make direct contact with people who have the authority to hire someone with your skills, even if they don't have a job opening now.

With this in mind, browse through the sample resumes that follow. All of them are based on real ones, but the content has been modified to protect the innocent. All were written by members of the Professional Association of Resume Writers, and these are credited as appropriate. The notes, of course, are mine.

Which brings me to one final comment: A professional resume writer can help you greatly, if you find the right one. Any secretarial service can type or "wordprocess" your resume so that it looks okay, but professional resume writers often include valuable counseling, writing, and design skills in their services. Members of the Professional Association of Resume Writers adhere to a code of ethics and have to pass a rigorous knowledge test. I recommend them. A good resume writer will charge more than a typing service, but you will get more in return. But whether you do it yourself or have help, the important thing is to get your resume out of the way, so you can get on with your active job search.

THIS RECENT GRAD PRESENTS HIS PART-TIME AND SUMMER JOBS VERY NICELY — AS PART OF HIS "PROFESSIONAL" WORK EXPERIENCE.

Mark T. Bradley, B.S.

9275 Catalpa • New Holland, Michigan 48337
(612) 555-9617

INTERESTING USE OF CLIP ART →

PROFILE:

Background of proven success in *Hospitality Management* including food and beverage control in various hotel and resort establishments. Experience features involvement with fine dining facilities in a 4 star, 4 diamond hotel, banquet facilities, and corporate fast food operations. Customer service a priority.

EDUCATION:

NOT INCLUDING A DATE AVOIDS DISPLAY OF A RECENT DEGREE.

College of Business, B.S. Hospitality Management, A.A.S. Diversified Business
Ferris State University, Big Rapids, Michigan

SUMMARY OF SKILLS AND TRAINING:

- Hire, train, schedule, and supervise up to 25 employees
- Develop advertising/marketing strategies
- Assist in determining menu selections stressing variety and utilizing seasonal foods
- Handle cost controls (food and labor), inventory controls, pricing, and purchasing
- Ensure all sanitation standards are being met including city, state, and federal codes
- Prepare and submit forecasting for financial and management matters
- Define goals for day to day operations
- Assist guests with room registration providing personalized service maximizing revenue and customer satisfaction
- Perform room service operations
- Set up and served banquets to 600 people
- Utilize computer for audits, reports, scheduling, etc.

PROFESSIONAL EXPERIENCE:

AGAIN, NOT INCLUDING DATES AVOIDS HIS DISPLAYING "LACK" OF EXPERIENCE

Manager
Pizza Hut, South Haven, Michigan

Internship
Amway Grand Plaza Hotel, Grand Rapids, Michigan (Front Desk)
Marriotts Marco Island Resort, Marco Island, Florida (Room Service and Banquets)

Bellhop/Room Service
Clarion Hotel & Conference Center, Big Rapids, Michigan

RELATED PROFESSIONAL ACTIVITIES:

- Purchasing Committee Chairman 1994 Annual Gala
- Training Intervention Procedures by Servers of Alcohol (TIPS)
- Front Office Procedures Certificate
- SYSCO Frost Pack Food Show, New Holland, Michigan

Submitted by: Patricia L. Nieboer, CPS, CPRW
The Office
25 W. Main St. B
Fremont, Michigan 49412-1135
Phone: (616) 924-6600   Fax: (616) 924-6694

PRESENTS VOLUNTEER AND LIFE EXPERIENCES HERE NICELY TO SUPPORT A TRANSITION TO AN ENTRY-LEVEL JOB WORKING WITH CHILDREN.

JENNIFER A. BLOOM

2236 East Oak Drive
Windfall, IN 46076
(317) 555-7649

PROFILE

A GOOD USE OF ADAPTIVE SKILLS HERE. IT WORKS WELL!!

Seeking a position working with children / providing office support in a day care or preschool setting. Responsible, dependable employee. Possess good interpersonal skills, and relate well to children.

RELEVANT VOLUNTEER EXPERIENCE

Preschool Teacher, Carroll Christian Church, Carroll, IN   9/90 - Present

WHY NOT? THIS IS GOOD INFORMATION TO INCLUDE HERE AS IT SUPPORTS HER JOB OBJECTIVE

Teach Sunday school to four-year-old children. Create a warm, relaxed learning environment for seven preschool students. Utilize the "time out" discipline approach. Plan lessons and craft projects appropriate for the season. Lead sing-a-long sessions; read Bible stories. Make progress reports to parents, and make recommendations to parents for home study. Plan and coordinate holiday parties.

Volunteer, at home   9/93 - Present

Assist my handicapped sister daily in special exercises and activities as directed by the occupational therapist from the Hope Treatment Center. Follow directions carefully and report results on a weekly basis.

CUSTOMER SERVICE EXPERIENCE

Provide polite, cheerful service to customers. Bag groceries, do price checks, and handle overstock. Help handicapped people do their shopping. Regularly complimented by customers for courteous service.

Received Kroger's commendation award for service above and beyond the ordinary.

OFFICE SUPPORT EXPERIENCE

Delivered medical records and charts, handled light typing, and filed records and charts.
Greeted customers, provided information, and opened safety-deposit accounts.

WORK HISTORY

Service Clerk	KROGER FOODS INC. Carroll, IN	10/91 - Present
Service Clerk	KROGER FOODS INC. Windfall, IN	4/86 - 10/91
Vault Clerk	WINDFALL STATE BANK Windfall, IN	5/84 - 4/86
Medical Records Clerk	TIPTON COUNTY MEDICAL CENTER Tipton, IN	6/80 - 5/84

EDUCATION

Tipton High School, Tipton, IN • GRADUATE

Hoosier Community College, Carroll, IN
Courses in continuing education • Earned certificate in BASIC COMPUTER OPERATIONS.

References will be provided upon request.

Submitted by: Jennie R, Dowden
Jenn's Resume Service
Flossmore, Illinois 60422
Phone: (708) 957-5976

WHILE THIS RESUME IS TARGETED TO HEALTHCARE, IT COULD EASILY BE RE-FOCUSED TO MORE GENERAL FINANCIAL MANAGEMENT POSITIONS.

Robert H. Colombo

18 Milton Lane • Needham, MA 01532
(617) 444-6631

Objective

To obtain a position as a *Financial Manager* in the Health Care industry utilizing 16 years of demonstrated success and accomplishment.

Summary

- Outstanding knowledge and expertise in Health Care with particular emphasis in analyzing and resolving financial problems.
- Effectively reorganized a $20 million agency realizing a significant increase in Federal reimbursements.
- Excellent knowledge and experience in all phases of financial management including operations, financial reporting, internal controls, controllership and financial analysis.
- Achieved outstanding results through tenacious and persistent application of sound financial management techniques.
- Demonstrated ability to effectively lead and develop a skilled staff.
- Able to successfully manage multiple priorities and assignments.
- Approach problems in a highly creative and effective manner.

Experience
1992 to Present

INTERNATIONAL HEALTH SPECIALISTS, INC., Newton, MA
Controller

- Significantly reduced A/R (mostly with 120 day aging) through controls, staffing changes, MIS additions, and management direction.
- Designed and implemented more informative P&L reports for growing divisions of healthcare services.
- Responsible for Accounting, Billing, Collections, Payroll, MIS and Accounts Payable.

1987 to 1992

DIGITAL EQUIPMENT CORPORATION, Marlboro, MA
Finance Manager - U.S. Leasing and Remarketing (8/89 to Present)
Administrative Finance Manager - U.S. Sales (6/88 - 8/89)
Sales Finance Manager - Southern Area (4/87 - 6/88)

EFFECTIVE USE OF CAPITAL LETTERS, BOLD FACE, ITALIC AND BULLETS — A SIMPLE, BUT EYE CATCHING TOUCH.

- Developed and implemented a Performance Reporting System that is able to effectively evaluate the quality of sales and to keep the performance of the division on track to accomplish stated goals.
- Successfully implemented the Leasing Business Plan with total sales volume of $400 million accounting for 10% of all sales at DEC.
- Conducted financial analysis of all new U.S. Sales Administration programs.
- Conducted Profit & Loss performance analysis to determine sales trends.
- Accurately and effectively completed monthly sales forecasts, developed an ongoing quarterly book, and coordinated third balance sheet review for operations.
- Hire, train and develop a staff of 10 professionals.

Robert H. Colombo
Page Two

1986 to 1987   SAMSON & SAMSON, Needham, MA
Senior Consultant
• Accountable for consolidations and mergers in the health care field.
Analyzed financial statements, conducted audits and prepared cost
reports.

1983 to 1986   BOSTON AFFILIATES, Boston, MA
Chief Financial Officer/Controller
• Full financial responsibility for this $22 million agency including
accounting, credits and collections and data control. Also managed
the Administrative Services which included purchasing and MIS.
Responsible for a staff of 50. Reported to the Executive Director.
• Effectively reorganized the agency resulting in a substantial increase
in Federal reimbursements. Realized a 20% savings through
inventory controls and competitive purchasing techniques.
• Successfully conducted Labor negotiations involving union employees
in 5 locations. Conducted rental/lease contract negotiations.

1980 to 1983   VISITING NURSE ASSOCIATION OF WORCESTER, INC.
Worcester, MA
Controller
• Responsible for the total Financial Management of the Association.
Achieved a stabilized financial position and provided guidance to the
Executive Director and Board of Directors.

1974 to 1980   MILFORD WHITINSVILLE REGIONAL HOSPITAL, Whitinsville, MA
General Accountant

Education   Bryant College, Smithfield, RI
M.B.A. 1982.
B.S. in Accounting. 1975.

SUPERIOR CREDENTIALS THAT MIGHT JUSTIFY MORE DETAILS, THOUGH HIS SUBSTANTIAL EXPERIENCE MAKES IT LESS IMPORTANT.

Community Activites
• *Treasurer* and Board Member, Massachusetts Association of
Community Health Agencies (MACHA);

• *Chairman* of the Regulatory Committee of MACHA.

--REFERENCES AVAILABLE UPON REQUEST--

Submitted by: Steven Green, CPRW
Career Path
242 Brewer Street
Northboro, Massachusetts 01532
Phone: (508) 393-5548

EMPHASIZES WHAT SHE CAN OFFER

JANE HALE

A NICE JOB FOR A ONE PAGE RESUME!

39-11 Briarwood Lane • Marlboro, MA 01752
(508) 624-7349

OBJECTIVE

To obtain a position as an *Elementary School Teacher* in which a strong dedication to the total development of children and a high degree of enthusiasm can be fully utilized.

EXPERIENCE
9/90 to Present

Mary Finn School, Southboro, MA
First Grade Teacher

A NICE GRAPHIC TOUCH

- Participated in the design and development of a **Whole Language Reading** curriculum that included large and small group instruction. Participated in the development of assessment tools to evaluate Whole Language.
- Adapted the Whole Language Program to meet individual needs by using elements of a basal and/or a phonetic reading program.
- Implemented DMP (**Developmental Math Process**) which is a hands on approach to problem solving through the use of math manipulatives.

THIS APPROACH ALLOWS HER TO PROVIDE A LOT OF DETAIL FOR JUST ONE JOB — AND DO SO IN AN INTERESTING WAY

- Developed learning centers based on the needs of a heterogeneous class. Utilized a **thematic approach** to the curriculum.
- Have stressed an individual approach to learning by providing enrichment as well as modification based on a particular student's needs.
- Participated in organizing curriculum units including **Chinese New Year**, **Ecology**, and **Weather**.
- Fostered ongoing communication with parents through the use of a monthly newsletter detailing thematic units.
- Involved parent volunteers to assist the children in classroom enrichment activities such as the use of computers and numerous whole class projects.
- Contributing member of Building Based Support Team pilot program, a 3 year grant funded by the State Department of Education.

COLLEGE RELATED TEACHING ASSIGNMENTS
Fall 1989

Mary Finn School, Southboro, MA
First Grade--Student Teacher.

EMPHASIZES ACCOMPLISHMENTS

- Developed teaching units on the seashore and trees, and utilized advanced teaching methods including Whole Language and math manipulatives. Developed and implemented learning centers.

Spring 1989

Warren School, Ashland, MA
Second Grade--Field Study II.
- Developed plans for individual and group use on Time and Money.

Fall 1988

Framingham State College Nursery School, Framingham, MA
To Fulfill Requirements for Curriculum I.
- Developed extensive observation and management skills.

Spring 1988

Lilja Elementary School, Natick, MA
First Grade--Field Study I; Teachers Aide

EDUCATION

Framingham State College, Framingham, MA
B.S., Early Childhood Education. Minor: Psychology. 1990.
Workshop: American Sign Language. Sponsored by Mary Finn School.

AWARDS AND ACHIEVEMENTS

Dorothea J. Kunde Memorial Award For Excellence In Teaching 1989-1990.
President's List, 1989-1990; Dean's List, 1988-1990.

Submitted by: Steven Green, CPRW
Career Path
242 Brewer Street
Northboro, Massachusetts 01532
Phone: (508) 393-5548

SUSAN WHITAKER
1227 Juniper Drive
Bloomington, Indiana 47401
(812) 555-9445

HIGHLIGHTS OF QUALIFICATIONS

- Four years experience in administrative/clerical support positions.
- Easily establish rapport with managers, staff, and customers.
- Proficient at analyzing statistics and market trends to develop accurate forecasts and effective sales presentations.
- Excellent problem solving, project management and decision making skills.
- Proven ability to prioritize and complete multiple tasks.

COMPUTER SKILLS

Software:	WordPerfect, Microsoft Word for Windows
Graphics:	Harvard Graphics, Powerpoint for Windows
Database:	Telemagic
Hardware:	Apple IIE, HP and most IBM compatibles
Spreadsheets:	Lotus 1-2-3, Microsoft Excel, Quattro Pro

[handwritten: IMPORTANT DETAILS TO EMPHASIZE]

OFFICE SKILLS

65+ wpm typing, 75 wpm word processing, 70+ wpm shorthand, CRT, dictation, 10-key adding machine, statistical analysis

PROFESSIONAL EXPERIENCE

PEPSI-COLA COMPANY, Indianapolis, Indiana   1988 - Present
Administrative Assistant

- Analyze sales volume and profit.
- Finalize and package forecasting reports for more than $100 million in annual sales.
- Monitor monthly spending and reconciliation for $8 million budget.
- Manage $300,000 in advertising and promotional materials.
- Interact with sales staff impacting service to 1200 customers.

[handwritten: EVERY LINE INCLUDES SOME NUMBERS]

EDUCATION

Executive Secretarial Certificate, 1988
ITT TECHNICAL INSTITUTE, Indianapolis, Indiana
- Dean's List, 3.7/4.0 GPA
- Maintained perfect attendance record

[handwritten: EXCELLENT DETAILS TO ADD!!]

REFERENCES AVAILABLE UPON REQUEST

Submitted by: John A. Suarez, CPRW
The Impact Group
7935A Clayton Road
St. Louis, Missouri 63117-1373
Phone: (314) 721-3900 • Fax: (314) 721-5805

This resume presents substantial experience by using brief, well-selected statements.

JESSIE W. FOLGER

783 Calhoon Drive
Greencastle, Indiana 46305
(317) 635-8824

EXPERTISE: **PURCHASING / MATERIALS MANAGER**

EXPERIENCE:

Simple, short statements. But they present him well →

Cast Metal Products, Inc., Greencastle, Indiana   3/88-Present

PURCHASING AGENT: Organize, manage, and supervise purchasing department for $30,000,000 manufacturer of die cast aluminum transmission housings.

ACCOMPLISHMENTS/PRIMARY FUNCTIONS:
- Consistently obtain 3%-5% annual cost reduction from vendors.
- Certified Instructor, "Working" Class; increase productivity/worker efficiency daily.
- Member, National Association of Purchasing Managers.
- Negotiate contracts for major commodities; emphasis in $23,000,000 of aluminum annually.
- Cost analysis for numerous items.
- Quality Circle Team Leader, commitment of team leadership/management philosophy.
- Extensive customer relations experience.
- In-depth knowledge of daily workings in manufacturing operation.

Myers Electric Equipment Company, Martinsville, Indiana   6/87-3/88

OUTSIDE ELECTRICAL SALES ENGINEER: Extensive customer interaction for major electrical distributor with four divisions.

ARCO Electric Products Corporation, Martinsville, Indiana   1/76-5/87

VICE PRESIDENT, CUSTOMER RELATIONS: Designed product compatibility systems for consumer needs. In-house and on-site troubleshooting application and engineering assistance.
VICE PRESIDENT, MARKETING: Administered guidance to 23 field agents. Developed new product literature.
NATIONAL SALES MANAGER: Ensured continuity of policies and practices for nationwide distribution market. Developed and implemented training program for representatives.
PURCHASING AGENT/BUYER: Improved inventory control system. Analyzed bids from different suppliers. Assessed and selected raw materials for use in all aspects of production.

EDUCATION:

Bachelor of Science, Education, Indiana University, Bloomington, Indiana

Continuing Education:
- Advanced Purchasing Strategies, Cast Metal Products, Inc.
- Successfully completed three in-house training programs, Cast Metal Products, Inc.
- Dale Carnegie, Simon D. Yancy Associates, Indianapolis, Indiana
- Accounting I, Indiana Vocational Technical College, Indianapolis, Indiana

CIVIC ACTIVITIES:

- Immediate Past President, Kiwanis Marks Club of Greencastle
- Member, Board of Directors, Brothers, Inc. of Morgan County
- Sub-committee Chairman, Partners-in-Education, Monroe County Chamber of Commerce
- Member, Monroe County Chamber of Commerce

Submitted by: Carole Pefley, CPRW
TESS, Inc.
6314 Morenci Trail, Suite 200
Indianapolis, Indiana 46268
Phone: (317) 291-3574 • Fax: (317) 291-3640

A GOOD APPEARANCE AND LAYOUT TO THIS MODIFIED CHRONOLOGICAL RESUME.

Jane E. Doe

P.O. Box 666 - Towny, Illinois 62222 - (217) 555-0000

SUMMARY OF QUALIFICATIONS:

- Strong accounting and recordkeeping aptitude experience.

- Effective planning and organization skills.

- Ability to work well both independently and in a team environment.

A NICE TOUCH

- Takes great pride in completing a job with accuracy, proficiency and effectiveness.

EXPERIENCE:
FROM HERE ON, THIS IS A TRADITIONAL CHRONOLOGICAL RESUME

March 1988 to December 1993	JOE'S BUILDING, INC., Towny, Illinois **Office Manager** Responsible for managing all accounts receivable, accounts payable, order entry, inventory, purchase order receivings and general ledger transactions utilizing the Great Plains Accounting System on an IBM compatible computer. Balanced manual checkbook to reconcile bank statements. Handled multi-line phone for customer inquiries, organized filing system and balanced cash drawer completing deposits.
April 1985 to February 1988	TOWNY ENERGY, Towny, Illinois **Secretary** Maintained employee payroll and tax records. Responsible for entire paper trail of business including accounts payable and receivable. Provided customer service by scheduling appointments and answering telephone questions. Utilized Apple computer.
October 1984 to April 1985	JILL'S FAST FOOD, Towny, Illinois **Assistant Head Cashier** Maintained daily deposits and balances of all cash registers. Opened and closed the store. Accountable for office paper trail of daily balances.
August 1976 to April 1984	GROCER'S, Towny, Illinois **Cashier/Office Assistant** Customer service representative through phone inquiries and office work. Relied on to close and balance cash registers and to make daily deposits.

EDUCATION:
HER ACADEMY, Towny, Illinois
Diploma

GREAT PLAINS ACCOUNTING SYSTEM, Poorboy, Texas
Certificate

REFERENCES:
Available upon request.

Submitted by: Laura G. Lichtinstein
Lasting Impressions Resume & Writing Service
Springfield, Illinois 62701
Phone: (217) 528-5782 • Fax: (217) 528-5579

A VERY EASY TO READ RESUME WITH A CLEAN FORMAT

S. OLIVIA HANSON
4444 Kitz Road
Evansville, Indiana 47711
(812) 555-5555

PROFILE

Highly skilled Executive Secretary with outstanding, professional experience including:

STRONG STATEMENTS OF ABILITIES — A GOOD OPENING

▸ Ability to communicate with all levels of management and employees.
▸ International communication liaison with subsidiary companies.
▸ Contract Negotiation Bargaining Team member.
▸ Use of word processing, windows and training on Lotus 1-2-3.

EXPERIENCE

PIONEER CORPORATION Evansville, Indiana
Executive Secretary 5/88 - 8/93
- Served as secretary to the Director of Plant Operations and to the Director of Engineering.
- Assisted in start-up of two branches of the company (Brazil, S.A., Ft. Smith, AR).
- Arranged all aspects of international and domestic travel for Engineering Department.
- Member of bargaining unit representing the Company during contract negotiations.
- Maintained executive calendars, scheduled appointments, and fielded phone calls.
- Prepared draft of monthly reports regarding current capital engineering projects.
- Routed all incoming company mail to appropriate department.
- Assisted in the preparation and editing of the company newsletter.
- Provided visitor assistance and arranged departmental luncheons.

SEIGNMAN ENGINEERING Evansville, Indiana
Part-Time Secretary/Receptionist 1983 - 1985
- Assisted with compiling legal data and putting it in chronological order.
- Prepared court exhibits.
- Typed correspondence and legal documents.
- Answered phones and greeted clients.

CENTRAL SERVICE Evansville, Indiana
Customer Service Representative 1978 - 1980
- Located overages/shortages at main store.
- Answered service calls, scheduled appointments, and resolved customer complaints.
- Performed clerical and cashier duties.

PET MEDICAL CENTER Evansville, Indiana
Veterinarian Assistant 1972 - 1978
- Assisted in surgery with anesthesia and instruments.
- Provided pre- and post-operative animal care.
- Performed administrative clerical and reception duties.

EDUCATION

INDIANA VOCATIONAL TECHNICAL COLLEGE Evansville, Indiana
Professional Secretary Certification November 1993

References Available Upon Request

Submitted by: Teresa Collins, CPRW • Erica Hanson
Quality Résumé
600 North Weinbach, Suite 810
Evansville, Indiana 47711
Phone: (812) 479-8380 • Fax: (812) 473-4892

THIS RESUME PRESENTS MR. RILEY AS IF SOMEONE ELSE WAS PRESENTING HIS BACKGROUND — AN INTERESTING APPROACH.

PROFESSIONAL PROFILE

CHARLES B. RILEY, CEI/CES

BACKGROUND

Charles B. Riley has had over 25 years of diversified experience in the technical and engineering field. His qualifications include having worked in Manufacturing/Industrial Management, Engineering Sales and Management; in addition to his positions as a Management Consultant Engineer, Safety Director, and more recently, Environmental Consultant.

PROFESSIONAL EXPERIENCE

A Professional Environmental Consultant since 1988, Mr. Riley specializes in the marketing of services related to:

- Contamination Assessments and Remediation at Hazardous and Non-hazardous sites.
- Underground Storage Tank (UST) Evaluations.
- Phase I, II and III Assessments.
- Asbestos Abatement/Radon Testing.
- OSHA 40-Hour Haz-Met School.
- Personnel Placement of Engineers and Technicians.

Mr. Riley's professional background includes prior employment with the following companies:

NOTICE THAT NO DATES ARE INCLUDED. THIS ALLOWS HIM TO PRESENT HIS EXPERIENCE WITHOUT DISPLAYING HIS AGE

Donahue Groover & Associates, Staff Engineer/Consultant. Coordinated financial budget (P&E); marketing and logistics; Industrial Relations; general overall monitoring of organizational activities.

INA Insurance Company of North America (now Cigna), Senior Marketing Technical Representative. Responsible for monitoring total loss control, in conjunction with 30 insurance agencies. Instructed insurance officials, their insureds, and prospective clients on the OSHA Regulations and the implementation of safety programs to insure governmental compliance.

Hayes Aircraft, Senior Project Engineer. Supervised eight engineers. Coordinated research and design problems on Saturn V Swing Arms. Worked closely with NASA Engineers in reviewing and resolving problem areas.

Bendix Corporation, Supervisor of 50 personnel at John F. Kennedy Space Center, Florida. Coordinated refurbishment of Saturn V Swing Arm. Supported NASA Contractors and directed all operations. Training instructor for mechanical and pneumatic personnel in Swing Arm project. Instructor at Ground School for Heavy Equipment and Launch Control Systems.

Honeywell, Inc., Industrial Engineer/Cost Estimator. Worked on various "classified assemblies" and military electronic devices. Prepared cost estimates for bidding.

EDUCATION

Mr. Riley studied Industrial Engineering at Ohio University and is also a graduate of the International Safety Academy. In July, 1992, he received a 40-Hour OSHA Certification from the Technical Environmental Training Institute. During his career, he has participated in a variety of certified, specialized training and management programs; together with being an instructor for a Welding School and the Saturn V Ground Support School. He has conducted seminars and given speeches on OSHA Regulations and Procedures; Safety Programs to Insure Compliance with OSHA; Environmental Work - Air Quality, Smoke Stack Emissions, and Water Contamination.

PROFESSIONAL MEMBERSHIPS/AFFILIATIONS

- Environmental Asssessment Association (EAA)
- Environmental Conservation Organization (ECO)
- Lifetime Member - Methods Time Management Association (MTM)

Submitted by: Diane McGoldrick
Business Services of Tampa Bay
10014 N. Dale Mabry Hwy. #101
Tampa, Florida 33618
Phone: (813) 968-3131 • Fax: (813) 960-9558

Susan Steinfeld

12 Browertown Road
Little Falls, NJ 07424
(201) 785-3011

GOOD USE OF WHITE SPACE

Objective

Senior administrative management position with an innovative company, where the professional execution of their special events and various marketing programs will be valued.

Personal Profile

Entrepreneurial, creative manager with strong leadership and motivational skills; extremely service oriented; unique combination of intuitive and analytical abilities; astute at recognizing areas in need of improvement, with the vision to develop action steps and see them through to a prompt and successful completion, well within budgetary framework; knowledge of conversational French.

Areas of Expertise

Special Event/Meeting Planning

- Eleven years of experience in the start to finish management of high budgeted, multi-faceted projects for the hospitality, franchise and other industries.

- Demonstrated exceptional ability to plan and organize a broad range of considerations from site negotiations to finishing details and amenities, with the style and panache befitting events such as grand openings, major conferences, fundraisers and employee/corporate functions.

- Screen and select agency personnel, freelancers and in-house staff, promoting harmonious working relationships throughout entire event staging process. Scope of involvement includes: coordination of attendees and presentors, travel/accommodations planning, theme-oriented decor, room set-up, food and beverage services, entertainment, audio-visual productions, and more.

Marketing Communications

- Heavy exposure to the entire creative execution of corporate marketing plans, guided only by minimal directives from management.

- Contract for and direct the activities of implementation teams which include: communications consultants, print and audio-visual production houses, photographers, artists, designers and public relations agencies, in addition to internal support staff, to produce creative promotional materials reflective of the corporate image.

- Awarded recognition for multiple print and other corporate communications pieces such as annual reports, franchise brochures, videos, consumer information bulletins, and company newsletters.

... Continued

Professional Experience

HOST SERVICES INTERNATIONAL, New York, NY   1991-Present

Director of Event Marketing for hotel property franchisor controlling 2500+ Howard Johnson's, Days Inn and Ramada facilities. Report to Executive Vice President of Marketing. Responsible for planning and executing major special events including annual conferences, cause related marketing, corporate meetings, and creative contributions to marketing plans.

- Within six months, orchestrated two successful major meetings normally requiring two years from inception of plans.
- Utilized economics of scale to produce two corporate functions with similar themes, back to back at the same location, saving the company at least $500,000 had they taken place at different times of the year.

BILLY BOB'S CHUCKWAGON, INC., Houston, TX   1981-1991

Director of Marketing Communications Services (1988-91) at Corporate Headquarters of $1.4 billion, 2400+ unit international restaurant chain.

- Reported to the Vice President of Corporate Communications and managed a staff of four in the areas of corporate communications/public relations, special events, publications, audio-visuals, and large scale meetings. Controlled a $1.2MM meeting budget.
- Promoted through the ranks of the marketing organization to director post by proving ability to take charge of problem areas and effect beneficial solutions.
  ... Initiated marketing information center to answer various inquiries from individual franchise operators; published a quarterly directory listing contacts for available services.
  ... Facilitated distribution of newly introduced but difficult to obtain marketing items. Traced cause of problem to short term lack of inventory and developed monitoring system to prevent recurrences.
  ... Took over meeting planner responsibility upon former incumbent's resignation three months before annual convention. With brand new management, developed and executed plans quickly, smoothly and to their satisfaction.
- Assumed permanent charge of event planning for the next seven years, each year progressively improving it with regard to increased attendance, quality of service and graphic design.
- Received Billy Bob's Outstanding Performance Award (four years) for quality and prompt execution of projects and recognition for award-winning annual reports.

Education

McGill University, Montreal, Canada (1975-77). Major in Marketing and Advertising. Management and Creative Writing seminars while at Billy Bob's.

Memberships

Meeting Planners, Inc.
Women in Communications

References and portfolio available upon request.

(handwritten note:) CHRONOLOGICAL LISTING OF JOBS GOOD INCLUDES EMPHASIS ON RESULTS

Submitted by: Melanie Noonan, CPS
Peripheral Pro
West Paterson, New Jersey
Business: Little Falls, New Jersey
Phone: (210) 785-3011 • Fax: (201) 785-3071

THIS GRAPHIC IS NOT THE ONLY INTERESTING FEATURE ON THIS RESUME. THE SIMPLE "HERE ARE THE FACTS" PRESENTATION WORKS VERY WELL HERE FOR THIS JOB OBJECTIVE

GARY D. RIETER
1210 Shore Lane, Elkhart,ID 46524
Phone (209) 634-4261

JOB OBJECTIVE: *Pilot position*

RATINGS/CERTIFICATES

Airline Transport Pilot - Multiengine
Commercial - Single Engine Land
Commercial - Single Engine Sea
Certified Flight Instructor
Certified Flight Instructor (Instrument)
Medical Certificate: FAA Class I - No Restrictions

FLIGHT TIME:

Total Flight Time	2683		Total Alaska Time	1000
Pilot in Command	1800		Instrument	250
Multiengine Land	412		Instrument Simulator	50
Single Engine Land	600		Military Flight Engineer	829
Single Engine Sea	810			

QUALIFICATIONS

Owner-Operator Line Pilot, Chief Flight Instructor and Company Safety Supervisor, Seahawk Air, Kodiak, Alaska, 1992-1993
Flight Engineer HC130H, U.S. Coast Guard, Florida & Alaska, 1989-1992. Safely logged 829 hours flight time. Member of Total Quality Management Team and Civil Rights Committee
Chief Flight Instructor, U.S. Coast Guard Flying Club, Kodiak, Alaska, 1990-1992. Implemented and monitored training and safety procedures
Flight Instructor, Keys Air Flight Training, Florida, 1989

SPECIALIZED TRAINING AND EDUCATION

Cockpit Resource Management, U.S. Air Force, completed annually 1987-1992
HC130H Advanced Electrical System, Dyess AFB, Texas, 1990
Basic & Advanced Flight Engineer, Little Rock AFB, Arkansas, 1989. Graduated top 10% of class. Course topics: turbine engine theory; systems - pressurization, bleed air, electrical, hydraulic, fuel, anti-ice, de-ice; and emergency procedures
University of Montana, Missoula, MT, 1982-1984

COMMUNITY AFFILIATIONS

Kodiak Civil Air Patrol, 1990-1992
Kodiak People for Pets (Humane Society)

References available upon request

Submitted by: Jacqueline K. Herter, CPS
Professional Word Processing
P.O. Box 3629
Kodiak, Alaska 99615
Phone: (907) 486-6221 • Fax: (907) 486-6267

105

A TRADITIONAL FORMAT THAT WAS TYPED ON A TYPEWRITER

KIM CHAN
88-35 Goodwill Boulevard, Apt. 3F
Bayside, New York 11355
(718) 444-7777

OBJECTIVE
Seeking a position as a Registered Nurse where I can be most
effective in helping other medical personnel assist patients and
provide quality health care.

EDUCATION
MANHATTAN COMMUNITY COLLEGE, New York, NY
Associates in Applied Sciences - Nursing, February, 1994
Curriculum included: Nursing Care Planning and Assessment,
Fundamentals of Nursing, Medical, Surgical, Pediatrics and Obstetrics
(68 credits) G.P.A.: 3.7

LICENSES
Registered Nurse - to sit for board March 1994
Licensed Practical Nurse - results pending from exam November 1993

PROFESSIONAL DEVELOPMENT
QUEENS HOSPITAL MEDICAL CENTER, Rosedale, NY   3/91 - Present
Transporter (3/93-present)
Transporting in-house patients to Radiology Department for CT,
Ultrasound and Nuclear Medicine. Work with OB/GYN patients, Cardiac
patients and bone fractures. This includes scanning for etopic
pregnancy, tumor diagnosis, etc. (To take time for school studies,
requested this part-time position).

Nursing Assistant (5/91-2/93)
Assisted Doctors and Nurses in the emergency room while attending to
various situations, i.e, accident victims, cardiac arrest, fractures,
etc. Responsible for taking blood pressure and temperature. Aided
Doctors while diagnosis was being made. (Full-time)

UNITED LANGUAGE SCHOOL, Bronx, NY   3/90 - 4/91
As a Chinese Instructor assisted English speaking lawyers who wanted
to learn Mandarin in order to be able to conduct business in the
Oriental community. Worked on a one-on-one basis. (Part-time)

QUEENS COUNTY HOSPITAL, Rego Park, NY   3/89 - 2/90
As an Interpreter worked with other medical practitioners to
determine the problems confronting patients admitted on various wards
throughout the facility. These patients were unable to speak good
English and many of the psychiatric patients were in a very confused
state of mind.

ADDITIONAL EDUCATION
SINGAPORE MEDICAL UNIVERSITY, Singapore, China   1984 - 1986
Completed four years of medical school curriculum which covered the
areas of internal medicine, general surgery, obstetrics, gynecology
and pediatrics. Received full scholarship and graduated with honors.
Credits received for basic medical courses were transferred to
Brooklyn Community College. Completed Medical Internship during the
fourth year at the Singapore Pie Jin and Singapore Da Pin Hospitals.

CERTIFICATE
CPR - American Heart Association, expiration date February 1993.

Submitted by: James Voketaitis
Resume Center of New York
39-15 Main Street, Suite 501
Flushing, New York 11354
Phone: (718) 445-1956 • Fax: (718) 445-1291

How to Get A Job NOW!

USES SMALL TYPE TO FIT ALL DETAILS ON TO ONE PAGE - BUT USE OF WHITE SPACE, BULLETS AND OTHER DESIGN FEATURES KEEP IT FROM LOOKING TOO "CROWDED".

Johanna Breitmorgan

2110 Sneckner Court
Morro Bay, California 90044
Telephone (213) 327-6111

Experience and education have provided detailed working knowledge of these key areas:

Financial Services	**Business Strategies**
Organization Development	**Customer Service**
Program Development	**Staffing & Training**
New Product Introductions	**Employee-Community Relations**

AN EFFECTIVE WAY TO PRESENT HER STRENGTHS

Highly motivated, results-oriented business professional with sixteen years of progressive accomplishments. Highly effective leadership skills, with an established track record of achievements. Fluent in French, German and English.

HANDLES SEVERAL POSITIONS WITH SAME EMPLOYER AS DIFFERENT JOBS

CRÉDITE INTERNATIONALE Morro Bay, California 1977 - Present
Have played key roles in managing change, building organizations, and working with senior management throughout this financial services organization that has 300 million cardholders in 240 countries and sales of $500 billion.

Director - Management Communications 1989 - Present
Partnering with the president and senior management of this 2,500-employee organization, created and launched programs for an executive speaker's bureau, employee communications, and community relations.

* Aggressively capitalized on opportunities and doubled the first year's number of speeches given by executive management; grew the total four-fold within three years.
* Developed and introduced a successful speech-merchandising program that, through press releases, op-ed articles, and reprints, delivered a strengthened image of Crédite as an industry leader.
* Developed a community relations program that made grant money available to non-profit organizations in which Crédite employees were working as volunteers.
* Recruited and worked closely with some 10 external speech writers.
* Planned and directed a complete re-design of the employee newsletter from improved graphics to an editorial planning calendar to meet the needs of multiple levels of management and staff.

Executive Assistant to the COO 1988 - 89
Pro-actively identified several significant corporate issues and, working with senior managers, developed plans to effect improvement.

* Resolved a growing problem of compliance between merchants and banks issuing the Crédite card.
* Revamped an out-moded mailing system to assure prompt delivery of important communications to banks.
* Prepared new policy and guidelines for employees to communicate with customers.

Director - Member Services 1985 - 88
Called in to manage a troubled, 35-employee unit that had an operating budget of $2 million and supported 80 major data centers, representing 1,500 banks, in the Western U.S. and Asia-Pacific.

* Restored high level of morale to the unit and reduced turnover to near zero.
* Managed and oversaw two complete changeovers in system software that enhanced productivity.

Earlier in member services (1981-85), presented trainings and seminars in the U.S. and Asia to enhance effectiveness and profitability of Crédite's computer systems.

Operations Coordinator 1979 - 81
Championed the development of an Fast-Pay Refund System when Crédite introduced travelers checks in 1982 and played a vital part in the worldwide implementation as liaison between the business unit and operations center.

Joined the company in Strasbourg, France, in 1977.

BA Degree - Psychology
STANFORD UNIVERSITY California

Submitted by: Ted Bache
Kingston-Bache Resumes
3130 Alpine Road, Suite 200-B
Portola Valley, California 94028
Phone: (415) 854-8594

THIS DEMONSTRATES THAT A ONE-PAGE RESUME CAN BE USED FOR AN EXECUTIVE POSITION.

ROBERT L. CARROLL
1670 Orange Grove Avenue
Winter Haven, Florida 32789
(407) 749-8381

OBJECTIVE

Seeking expanded opportunities within selected organizations where I can utilize my expertise to implement profit-oriented results.

PROFESSIONAL PROFILE

Extensive experience at the Senior Executive level in marketing multi-faceted services for a NASDAQ publicly-held company consisting of 53 drug store units, 6 home/health care convalescent centers, a drug store distribution center, 125 one-hour dry cleaning stores, a dry cleaning distribution center, and a manufacturing subsidiary of windows for drive-in service. Qualifications include a background in progressively responsible positions initiating from entry level management to CEO and President/Chairman of the Board. Established a successful history in the development and expansion of a diverse market reach resulting in a significant increase of annual gross revenues from $36 million to $80 million. Company was acquired by a national corporation in 1988.

EMPLOYMENT HISTORY

PHARMACEUTICAL/MANUFACTURING CO., Tampa, FL   **1993**
Director of Trade Relations / Assistant to the C.E.O.

> Public Relations and Corporate Marketing involving assimilation of conceptual and long-range planning strategies for a small, Bay-area, pharmaceutical/manufacturing company.

MANAGEMENT CONSULTANT, Knoxville, TN   **1988 - 1993**
Multiple Industries

> Provided consulting services to Retailers, Manufacturers and Distributors in the Southeast and Mid-West Territory of the U.S.

CARROLL ENTERPRISES, Lexington, KY   **1962 - 1988**

Chairman of the Board/President/CEO	1979-1988
President	1974-1979
Vice President - Advertising/Merchandising/Merchandise Distribution	1972-1974
Vice President - Drug Operations	1968-1972
Director of Merchandise / District Store Supervisor	1967-1968
Elected to Board of Directors	1967
Warehouse Manager / Seasonal & Promotional Buyer	1963-1967
Merchandise Manager	1962-1963

EDUCATION

UNIVERSITY OF CINCINNATI SCHOOL OF PHARMACY

UNIVERSITY OF KENTUCKY

PAST PROFESSIONAL AFFILIATIONS

Vice Chairman of the Board, Executive Committee Member, Board Member, Treasurer, Chairman of Finance Committee, and of Chairman of Government Affairs Committee for the **National Association of Chain Drug Stores (NACDS)**, Washington, D.C.

Chairman of Kentucky Retail Federation.

References and Detailed Resume Available Upon Request.

Submitted by: Diane McGoldrick
Business Services of Tampa Bay
10014 N. Dale Mabry Hwy. #101
Tampa, Florida 33618
Phone: (813) 968-3131 • Fax: (813) 960-9558

A·p·p·e·n·d·i·x C

Some Tips for Coping with Job Loss

Being out of work is not fun for most people, and it is devastating to some. It may help you to know you are not alone in this experience. I've included some information here on what to expect and some suggestions for getting through it.

Problems You May Encounter

Here are some feelings and experiences you may have after losing a job.

☼ **Loss of professional identity.** Most of us identify strongly with our careers, and unemployment often leads to a loss of self-esteem. Being employed

---

The material in this appendix is based on content from a book titled Job Strategies for Professionals, *written by a team of authors from the U.S. Employment Service (published by JIST).*

garners respect in the community and in the family. When a job is lost, part of your sense of self may be lost as well.

☼ **Loss of a network.** The loss is worse when your social life has been strongly linked to your job. Many ongoing "work friendships" are suddenly halted. Old friends and colleagues often don't call because they feel awkward or don't know what to say. Some don't want to be reminded of what could happen to them.

☼ **Emotional unpreparedness.** If you have never been unemployed before, you may not be emotionally prepared for it. You may feel devastated when it happens. It is natural and appropriate to feel this way. Some people you know might not take their job loss as hard as you have taken yours. Studies show that those who change jobs frequently and those who are in occupations prone to cyclic unemployment suffer far less emotional impact after job loss than those who have been steadily employed and who are unprepared for cutbacks.

Adjusting

Many studies have been done on dealing with loss. Psychologists have found that people often have an easier time coping with loss if they know what feelings they might experience during the "grieving process." Grief doesn't usually overwhelm us all at once; it is experienced in stages. The stages of loss or grief may include the following:

☼ **Shock:** You may not fully comprehend what has happened.

☼ **Denial:** You cannot believe the loss is true.

☼ **Relief:** You may feel a burden has been lifted and opportunity awaits.

☼ **Anger:** You blame (often without cause) those you think are responsible, including yourself.

☼ **Depression:** This may set in some time later, when you realize the reality of the loss.

☼ **Acceptance:** In this final stage of the process, you come to terms with the loss and get the energy and desire to move beyond it. The "acceptance" stage is the best place to be when starting a job search, but you may not have the luxury of waiting until this point to begin your search.

Knowing that most people will experience some predictable "grieving" reactions can help you deal with your loss in a constructive way. The faster you can begin an active search for a new job, the better off you will be.

Keep Healthy

Unemployment is a stressful time for most people, and it is important to stay healthy and fit.

☼ **Eat properly.** How you look and your sense of self-esteem can be affected by your eating habits. It's easy to snack on junk food when you're home all day. Take time to plan your meals and snacks so they are well-balanced and nutritious. Eating properly will help you maintain the good attitude you need during your job search.

☼ **Exercise.** Include some form of exercise as part of your daily routine. Regular exercise reduces stress and depression and can help you get through tough days.

☼ **Include time for fun.** When you're planning your time, be sure to build fun and relaxation into your plans. You are allowed to enjoy life even if you are unemployed. Keep a list of activities or tasks you want to accomplish, such as volunteer work, repairs around the house, or hobbies. When you have free time, you can refer to the list and have things to do.

Family Issues

Unemployment is hard on the entire family. For family members, your unemployment means loss of income and fear of an uncertain future. They are also worried about your happiness. Here are some ways you can help your family get through this tough time.

- ☼ **Don't attempt to shoulder your problems alone.** Be open with family members, even though it may be hard. Discussing your job search and the feelings you have allows your family to work as a group and support one another.
- ☼ **Talk to your family.** Let them know your plans and activities. Share with them how you will be spending your time.
- ☼ **Listen to your family.** Find out their concerns and suggestions. There may be ways they can help you.
- ☼ **Build family spirit.** You will need a great deal of support from your family in the months ahead, but they will also need yours.
- ☼ **Seek outside help.** Join a family support group. Many community centers, mental health agencies, and colleges have support groups for the unemployed and their families. These groups provide safe places to let off steam and share frustrations. They can also be sources of ideas on how to survive this difficult period. More information about support groups is presented later in this appendix.

Helping Children

Children can be deeply affected by a parent's unemployment. It is important for them to know what has happened and how it will affect the family. Be honest, but try not to overburden them with the responsibility of too many emotional or financial details.

- ☼ **Keep an open dialogue with your children.** It is vital to let them know what is really going on.

Children have a way of imagining the worst, so the facts are often far less devastating than what they envision.

☀ **Make sure your children know it's not anyone's fault.** Children may not understand job loss, and they may think that you did something wrong to cause it. Or they may feel that somehow *they* are responsible or financially burdensome. They need reassurance on these matters, regardless of their ages.

☀ **Children need to feel they are helping.** They want to help, and having them do something–like taking a cut in allowance, deferring expensive purchases, or getting an after-school job–can make them feel as if they are part of the team.

☀ **Get help at school.** Some experts suggest that you alert the school counselor to your unemployment so that he or she can watch the children for problems at school before the problems become serious.

Coping with Stress

Here are some coping mechanisms to help you deal with the stress of being unemployed.

☀ **Write down what seems to be causing the stress.** Identify your stressors, then think of possible ways to handle each one. Can some demands be altered, lessened, or postponed? Can you live with any of them just as they are? Are there some that you could deal with more effectively?

☀ **Set priorities.** Deal with the most pressing needs or changes first. You cannot handle everything at once.

☀ **Establish a workable schedule.** When you set a schedule for yourself, make sure it is one you can follow. As you perform your tasks, you will feel a sense of control and accomplishment.

☀ **Reduce your stress.** Learn relaxation techniques. These can be as simple as sitting in a comfortable chair, closing your eyes, taking deep breaths, and breathing out slowly while envisioning all the tension going out with your breath. There are a number of other methods, including listening to relaxation tapes, which may help you cope with stress more effectively. Check out additional materials that offer instruction on these techniques at your public library.

☼ **Avoid isolation.** Stay in touch with your friends–even former coworkers, if you can do so comfortably. Unemployed people often feel a sense of isolation and loneliness. See your friends, talk with them, socialize. You are the same person you were before your unemployment. The same goes for the activities you have enjoyed in the past. Evaluate them. Which can you afford to continue? If your old hobbies or activities can't be part of your new budget, maybe you can substitute new activities that are less costly.

☼ **Join a support group.** No matter how understanding or caring your family or friends are, they may not be able to understand all that you're going through. You might find help and understanding through a job seeking support group.

These groups are composed of people who are going through the same experiences and emotions that you are. Many groups also share tips on job opportunities, as well as feedback on job search methods. *The National Business Employment Weekly,* available at major newsstands, lists support groups throughout the country. Local churches, YMCAs, YWCAs, and libraries often list or facilitate support groups. A list of self-help organizations–some of which cover the unemployed–is available from the National Self-Help Clearinghouse, 25 West 43rd St., Room 620, New York, NY 10036. The list costs $3, plus a self-addressed, stamped envelope.

Forty Plus, a national nonprofit organization, is an excellent source of information about clubs

114

around the country and issues concerning older employees and the job search process. The address is 15 Park Row, New York, NY 10038. The telephone number is (212) 233-6086.

Keep Your Spirits Up

Here are some ways you can maintain your self-esteem and avoid depression.

- ☼ **List your positives.** Make a list of your positive qualities and your successes. It's easier to do this when you are feeling good about yourself. Enlist the assistance of a close friend or caring relative, or wait for a sunny moment.
- ☼ **Replay your positives.** Once you have made your list, replay it in your mind frequently. Associate the replay with something you do on a regular basis; for example, you might review the list in your mind every time you go to the refrigerator.
- ☼ **Go over the list before performing difficult tasks.** Review the list when you are feeling down or to give you energy before you attempt some difficult task.
- ☼ **Recall successes.** Take time every day to recall a success.
- ☼ **Use realistic standards.** Avoid the trap of evaluating yourself against impossible standards. You are in a particular phase of your life; don't dwell on what you think society regards as success. Remind yourself that success will come again.
- ☼ **Know your strengths and weaknesses.** What do you do well? What skills do you have? Do you need to learn new skills? Everyone has limitations. What are yours? Are there certain job duties that are just not right for you and that you might want to avoid? Balance your limitations against your strong skills so that you don't let the negatives eat at your self-esteem. Incorporate this knowledge into your career planning.

- ☼ **Picture success.** Practice visualizing positive outcomes before the event. Play out the scene in your imagination and picture yourself successful in whatever you're about to attempt.
- ☼ **Build success.** Make a "to do" list. Include small, achievable tasks. Divide the tasks and make a list for every day so you will have some "successes" daily.
- ☼ **Surround yourself with positive people.** Socialize with family and friends who are supportive. You want to be around people who will pick you up, not knock you down. You know who your fans are. Find time to be around them.
- ☼ **Volunteer.** Give something of yourself to others through volunteer work. Volunteering will help you feel worthwhile and may actually give you new skills.

Overcoming Depression

As hard as it is to be out of work, it also can be a new beginning. A new direction may emerge that will change your life in positive ways. This may be a good time to reevaluate your attitudes and outlook.

- ☼ **Live in the present.** The past is over and you cannot change it. Learn from your mistakes, and use that knowledge to plan for the future. Then let the past go. Don't dwell on it or relive it. Don't be overpowered by guilt.
- ☼ **Take responsibility for yourself.** Try not to complain or blame others. Save your energy for activities that result in positive experiences.
- ☼ **Learn to accept what you cannot change.** Don't waste your energy on things you can't change, but realize that in most situations, you *do* have some control. Your reactions and your behavior are in your control and will often influence the outcome of events.
- ☼ **Keep your job search under your own command.** This will give you a sense of control and prevent

you from simply giving up and waiting for something to happen. Enlist others' aid in your job search, but make sure *you* do most of the work.

- ☼ **Talk things out with people you trust.** Admit how you feel. If you recognize you're angry, find a positive way to vent it, perhaps through exercise.
- ☼ **Face your fears.** Try to pinpoint them. "Naming the enemy" is the best strategy for relieving vague feelings of anxiety. By facing what you actually fear you can determine if your fears are realistic.
- ☼ **Think creatively.** Stay flexible, take risks, and don't be afraid of failure. Try not to take rejection personally. Think of it as information that will help you later in your search. Take criticism as a way of learning more about yourself. Keep plugging away at the job search despite those inevitable setbacks. Most important, *forget magic*. What lies ahead is hard work!

Sources of Professional Help

If your depression won't go away, or if it leads you to self-destructive behaviors such as abuse of alcohol or drugs, consider asking a professional for help. Many people who have never sought professional help find that in a time of crisis it is crucial to have someone listen and give assistance. Consult a local mental health clinic, social services agencies, religious organizations, or professional counselors for help for yourself and family members who are affected by your unemployment. Your health insurance may cover some assistance. If you do not have insurance, many counselors determine their fees on a sliding scale based on income.

Managing Your Finances

Being unemployed has obvious financial consequences. While the best solution to this is to get a good job as soon as possible, you do need to manage your money differently during the time between jobs. Following are some things to think about.

Apply for Benefits Without Delay

Don't be embarrassed to apply for unemployment benefits as soon as possible, even if you're not sure you are eligible. This program is there to help you make a transition between jobs, and you helped pay for it during your previous employment. Depending on how long you have worked, you can collect benefits for up to 26 weeks, sometimes even longer. Contact your state labor department or employment security agency for further information. Their addresses and telephone numbers are listed in the phone book.

Prepare Now to Stretch Your Money

Being out of work means having a lower income. You need to control your expenses. The more you plan, the better you can control your finances.

Examine Your Income and Expenses

Create a budget and look for ways to cut your expenses. Filling out the Monthly Income and Expense Worksheet that follows can help you isolate income and expense categories, but your own budget may be considerably more detailed. I've included two columns for each expense category. In the "Normal" column, enter what you have been spending in each category during the time you were employed. In the "Could Reduce To" column, enter a lower number that you will spend by cutting expenses.

Monthly Income and Expense Worksheet

Income

Unemployment benefits	_____	Interest/Dividends	_____
Spouse's income	_____	Other income	
Severance pay	_____	TOTALS	_____

Expenses

	Normal	Could Reduce To		Normal	Could Reduce To
Mortgage/rent:	_____	_____		_____	_____
maintenance/				_____	_____
repairs	_____	_____		_____	_____
			Health insurance:	_____	_____
Utilities:			Other medical/		
electric	_____	_____	dental expenses	_____	_____
gas/oil heat	_____	_____			
water/sewer	_____	_____	**Tuition:**	_____	_____
telephone	_____	_____	other school costs	_____	_____
Food:	_____	_____	**Clothing:**	_____	_____
restaurants	_____	_____	**Entertainment:**	_____	_____
Car payment:	_____	_____	**Taxes:**	_____	_____
fuel	_____	_____	**Job hunting costs:**	_____	_____
maintenance/					
repairs	_____	_____	**Other expenses:**	_____	_____
insurance	_____	_____	**TOTALS**	_____	_____
Other loan payments:	_____	_____			

Tips on Conserving Your Cash

While you are unemployed, it is likely that your expenses will exceed your income, and it is essential that you be aggressive in managing your money. Your objective here is very clear: *You want to conserve as much cash as possible early on so you will have it for essentials later.* Here are some suggestions.

119

- ☼ **Begin cutting nonessential expenses right away.** Don't put this off! There is no way to know how long you will be out of work, and the faster you deal with the financial issues, the better.
- ☼ **Discuss the situation with family members.** Ask them to get involved by helping you identify expenses they can cut.
- ☼ **Look for sources of additional income.** Can you paint houses on weekends? Pick up a temporary job or consulting assignment? Deliver newspapers in the morning? Can a family member get a job to help out? Any new income will help, and the sooner the better.
- ☼ **Contact your creditors.** Even if you can make full payments for awhile, work out interest-only or reduced amount payments as soon as possible. When I was unemployed, I went to my creditors right away and asked them to help. They were very cooperative. Most are, if you are reasonable with them.
- ☼ **Register with your local consumer credit counseling organization.** Many areas have free consumer credit counseling organizations that will help you get a handle on your finances and encourage your creditors to cooperate.
- ☼ **Review your assets.** Make a list of all your assets and their current value. Money in checking, savings, and other accounts is the most available, but you may have additional assets in pension programs, life insurance policies, and stocks that could be converted to cash if needed. You may also have an extra car you could sell, equity in your home you could borrow against, and other assets you haven't thought of.
- ☼ **Reduce credit card purchases.** Try to pay for things with cash to save on interest charges and prevent overspending. Be disciplined. You can always use your credit cards later if you are getting desperate for food and other basics.

☼ **Consider cashing in "luxury" assets.** For example, sell a car or boat you rarely use to generate cash and to save on insurance and maintenance costs.

☼ **Comparison shop for home, auto, and life insurance and other expenses to lower costs.**

☼ **Deduct job hunting expenses from your taxes.** Some expenses may be tax deductible as "miscellaneous deductions" on your federal income tax return. Keep receipts for employment agency fees, resume expenses, and transportation expenses. If you find work in another city and you must relocate, some moving expenses are tax deductible. Contact an accountant or the IRS for more information.

Review Your Health Coverage

You already know that it is dangerous to go without health insurance, so there is no need to lecture you on this, but here are some tips.

☼ **You can probably maintain your coverage at your own expense.** Under the COBRA law, if you worked for an employer that provided medical coverage and had 20 or more employees, you can continue your health coverage. However, you must inform your former employer within 60 days of leaving the job.

☼ **Contact professional organizations to which you belong.** They may provide group coverage for members at low rates.

☼ **Speak to an insurance broker.** If necessary, arrange for health coverage on your own or join a local health maintenance organization (HMO).

☼ **Practice preventive medicine.** The best way to save money on medical bills is to stay healthy. Try not to ignore minor ills. If they persist, phone or visit your doctor.

☼ **Investigate local clinics.** Many local clinics provide services based on a sliding scale fee. These clinics often provide quality health care at affordable prices. In an emergency, most hospitals will provide you with services on a sliding scale fee, and most areas have one or more hospitals funded locally to provide services to those who can't afford them.

A·p·p·e·n·d·i·x

Bibliography— Sources of Job Leads and Other Information

If you've been to a large bookstore lately, you've probably noticed that there are many books in the "career" section. Each year, there are more books published on this topic and, unfortunately, most of them are not very good. I have listed here resources that are of particular importance to you in your job search. Of course, I have included many of the books I have written and many that are published by JIST–it seemed only fair. Most are available from a bookstore or good library.

Career Planning, Job Seeking, Resumes, and Career Success

Job Seeking and Interviewing

The Very Quick Job Search: Get a Better Job in Half the Time! (2nd Edition) by J. Michael Farr. This is my most thorough job search book, and it includes lots of information on career planning and, of course, job seeking. This is the book I would recommend to a friend who is out of work if I had to recommend just one. (JIST)

The Quick Interview & Salary Negotiation Book: Dramatically Improve Your Interviewing Skills in Just a Few Hours! by J. Michael Farr. This is a substantial book with lots of information, but it's arranged so you can read the first section, then go out and do better in interviews the same day. (JIST)

Getting the Job You Really Want A Step-by-Step Guide (3rd Edition) by J. Michael Farr. This one provides career planning and job search materials in a workbook format with lots of worksheets. It has sold more than 150,000 copies and counting. (JIST)

Career Satisfaction and Success: A Guide to Job and Personal Freedom by Bernard Haldane. This is a complete revision of a classic by one of the founders of the modern career planning movement. Not so much a job search book as a job *success* book. Contains solid information. (JIST)

Using the Internet and the World Wide Web in Your Job Search by Fred E. Jandt and Mary B. Nemnich. For new or experienced users of online computer services, this book gives lots of good information on finding job opportunities on the Web. (JIST)

The PIE Method for Career Success: A Unique Way to Find Your Ideal Job by Daniel Porot. Written by one of Europe's premier career consultants, this book presents powerful career planning and job seeking concepts in a visual and memorable way. (JIST)

Job Strategies for Professionals: A Survival Guide for Experienced White-Collar Workers by the U.S. Employment Service. Job search advice for professionals and managers who have lost their jobs. (JIST)

What Color Is Your Parachute? by Richard N. Bolles. This is the best-selling career planning book of all time, and the author continues to improve it. (Ten Speed Press)

The Complete Job Search Handbook: All the Skills You Need to Get Any Job, and Have a Good Time Doing It by Howard Figler. A very good book. (Henry Holt)

Who's Hiring Who? by Richard Lathrop. Another good book. (Ten Speed Press)

Job Hunters Sourcebook: Where to Find Employment Leads and Other Job Search Sources by Michelle LeCompte. (Gale Research)

Sweaty Palms Revised: The Neglected Art of Being Interviewed by Anthony Medley. (Ten Speed Press)

Dare to Change Your Job and Your Life by Carole Kanchier. Practical and motivating guidance on achieving career and personal growth and satisfaction. (JIST)

Resumes and Cover Letters

The Quick Resume & Cover Letter Book: Write and Use an Effective Resume in Only One Day by J. Michael Farr. Starting with an "instant" resume worksheet and basic formats that you can complete in an hour, this book takes you on a tour of everything you ever wanted to know about resumes and, more importantly, how to use them in your job search. (JIST)

The Resume Solution: How to Write (and Use) a Resume That Gets Results by David Swanson. Lots of good advice and examples for creating superior resumes. Very strong on design and layout, this book provides a step-by-step approach that is easy to follow. (JIST)

Gallery of Best Resumes: A Collection of Quality Resumes by Professional Resume Writers by David F. Noble. Advice and more than 200 examples from professional resume writers. With lots of variety in content and design, this is an excellent resource. I consider it the best resume "library" available. (JIST)

Gallery of Best Resumes for Two-Year Degree Graduates: A Special Collection of Quality Resumes by Professional Resume Writers by David F. Noble. A showcase of resumes written especially to help two-year degree graduates compete in the job market. (JIST)

Using WordPerfect in Your Job Search by David F. Noble. A unique and thorough book that reviews how to use the power of WordPerfect to create effective resumes, correspondence, and other job search documents. (JIST)

The Perfect Resume by Tom Jackson. (Doubleday)

Dynamite Cover Letters by Ron and Caryl Krannich. (Impact Publications)

Dynamite Resumes by Ron and Caryl Krannich. A good book. (Impact Publications)

The Damn Good Resume Guide by Yana Parker. Lots of good examples and advice. (Ten Speed Press)

Education, Self-Employment, and Starting a Business

Mind Your Own Business! Getting Started as an Entrepreneur by LaVerne Ludden and Bonnie Maitlen. A good book for those considering self-employment, with lots of good advice. (JIST)

Franchise Opportunities Handbook: A Complete Guide for People Who Want to Start Their Own Franchise by the U.S. Department of Commerce and LaVerne Ludden. Lists 1,500 franchise opportunities and information on selecting and financing a start-up. (JIST)

Back to School: A College Guide for Adults by LaVerne
   Ludden. Inside advice and valuable information for
   adults considering a return to school. (JIST)
Luddens' Adult Guide to Colleges and Universities by
   LaVerne Ludden and Marsha Ludden. Up-to-date
   information on more than 400 adult-friendly
   college and university programs in the U.S. (JIST)
*The Career Connection for College Education: A Guide to
   College Education & Related Career Opportunities* by
   Fred A. Rowe. Covers about 100 college majors and
   their related careers. (JIST)
*The Career Connection for Technical Education: A Guide to
   Technical Training & Related Career Opportunities* by
   Fred Rowe. Describes more than 60 technical
   education majors and the careers to which they
   lead. (JIST)

Information on Occupations and Industries

Occupational Outlook Handbook (OOH). Published every
   two years by the U.S. Department of Labor's Bureau
   of Labor Statistics, this book provides thorough
   descriptions of the 250 jobs that cover about 85
   percent of the workforce, including information on
   skills required, working conditions, duties, qualifications, pay, and advancement potential. Very helpful
   for preparing for interviews by identifying key skills
   to emphasize. (U.S. Department of Labor; JIST
   publishes a reprint)
America's Top 300 Jobs. JIST's bookstore version of the
   OOH. The *OOH* itself is typically kept in the
   reference section of the library, but this version,
   which can often be checked out, allows you to
   access the same information at your leisure. (JIST)
*Career Guide to America's Top Industries: Presenting Job
   Opportunities and Trends in All Major Industries* (2nd
   Edition). Provides trends and other information on

more than 40 major industries and summary data on many others. Includes details on employment projections, advancement opportunities, major trends, and a complete narrative description of each industry. (JIST)

The Complete Guide for Occupational Exploration (CGOE), edited by J. Michael Farr. Lists more than 12,000 job titles in a format that makes it easy to explore career alternatives or other jobs you may seek based on current skills. Jobs with similar characteristics are grouped together. The *CGOE* also cross-references to standard sources of additional information on the jobs it lists. (JIST)

The Enhanced Guide for Occupational Exploration (EGOE) (2nd Edition) compiled by Marilyn Maze and Donald Mayall. Using the same organizational structure as the *CGOE,* this book includes brief descriptions of about 2,800 jobs. Useful for career exploration, identifying skills used in previous jobs, researching new job targets, and preparing for interviews. (JIST)

Dictionary of Occupational Titles (DOT) (4th Edition Revised) by the U.S. Department of Labor. Provides descriptions for more than 12,000 jobs, covering virtually all jobs in our economy. This book can be used to identify jobs in different fields that use skills similar to those you have acquired in past jobs, identify key skills to emphasize in interviews, and much more. (U.S. Department of Labor, JIST publishes a reprint)

The Top Job Series. Each book in *America's Top Jobs™ Series* has a specific emphasis, providing thorough descriptions for the top jobs in a field, career planning and job search tips, plus details on growth projections, education required, and other data on 500 additional jobs. (JIST)

America's Fastest Growing Jobs

America's Federal Jobs

America's Top Office, Management, Sales & Professional Jobs

America's Top Medical, Education, & Human
    Services Jobs
America's Top Military Careers
America's Top Jobs™ for People Without College Degrees
America's Top Jobs™ for College Graduates
Dictionary of Occupational Terms: A Guide to the Special
    Language and Jargon of Hundreds of Careers by Nancy
    Shields. An interesting reference book that will
    answer most of your questions on more than 3,000
    terms. (JIST)

Information on Specific Organizations

Once you have a good idea of the industries, fields of
work, and geographical areas in which you want to
concentrate your job search, the next step is to locate
companies that might employ people in your field. Several
publications contain lists of companies by industry,
location, size, and other defining characteristics. A few of
them are discussed below.

The Job Hunter's Guide to 100 Great American Cities.
    Rather than concentrating on a particular locale,
    this guide gives the principal-area employers for 100
    of America's largest cities. (Brattle Communications)
Macrae's State Industrial Directories. Published for 15
    Northeastern states. Similar volumes are produced
    for other parts of the country by other publishers.
    Each book lists thousands of companies,
    concentrating almost exclusively on those that
    produce products rather than services. (Macrae)
National Business Telephone Directory. An alphabetical
    listing of companies across the United States, in-
    cluding addresses and phone numbers. This book
    includes many smaller firms. (Gale Research)
Thomas Register. Lists more than 100,000 companies
    across the country, including name, type of product
    made, and brand name of products. Catalogs

provided by many of the companies are included. (Thomas)

America's Fastest Growing Employers. Lists more than 700 of the fastest growing companies in the country. (Bob Adams)

The Hidden Job Market: A Guide to America's 2000 Little-Known Fastest Growing High-Tech Companies. Concentrates on high-tech companies with good growth potential. (Peterson's Guides)

Dun & Bradstreet Million Dollar Directory. Provides information on 180,000 of the largest companies in the country, including type of business, number of employees, and sales volume. Also lists the company's top executives. (Dun & Bradstreet)

Standard & Poor's Register of Corporations, Directors and Executives. Information similar to that in *Dun & Bradstreet's Million Dollar Directory.* Also contains a listing of the parent companies of subsidiaries and the interlocking affiliations of directors. (Standard & Poor)

The Career Guide: Dun's Employment Opportunities Directory. Aimed specifically at the professional job seeker, this directory lists more than 5,000 major U.S. companies which plan to recruit in the coming year. Lists personnel directors and information about firms' career opportunities and benefits packages. (Dun)

There are many directories that give information about firms in particular industries. A few samples are listed below:

The Blue Book of Building and Construction
Directory of Advertising Agencies
Directory of Computer Dealers
McFadden American Bank Directory

Your local chamber of commerce and business associations may also publish directories listing companies in your area. These are available in libraries or by writing to individual associations. And, of course, the *Yellow Pages* provide local listings of government and business organizations for every section of the country.

Professional and Trade Associations

These associations offer another avenue for getting information about where to find the type of work you want to do. These associations:

- ☼ Help you identify areas where growth is occurring.
- ☼ Provide the names of firms that employ people in a specific type of work.
- ☼ Identify the best information sources for developments within the field.
- ☼ Provide more information on leads in small firms than directories.
- ☼ Publish newsletters or journals that provide information on companies needing increased staff in the near future.

Some publications that list trade and professional associations are listed below.

Encyclopedia of Associations. Lists more than 22,000 professional, trade, and other nonprofit organizations in the United States. (Gale Research)

Career Guide to Professional Associations. Describes more than 2,500 professional associations. The information is more specifically oriented to the job seeker than is the *Encyclopedia of Associations*, but this guide has not been updated since 1980, and some of the information may not be current. (Garrett Park Press)

Newspapers

Newspapers contain want ads and lots of other useful employment information. Articles about new or expanding companies can be valuable leads for new job possibilities.

If relocating is a possibility, look at newspapers from other areas. They can serve as a source of job leads as well as give you some idea of the job market. The major out-of-town newspapers are sold in most large cities and are also available in many public libraries.

Some newspapers–such as *The New York Times, The Chicago Tribune*, and *The Financial Times*–are national in scope. *The National Business Employment Weekly*, published by *The Wall Street Journal*, contains information of interest to professional job seekers.

Networking

Networking is an excellent way of gathering information about a particular field. It is one of the best ways to discover smaller companies, which often are not listed in directories.

Computer Software

Any good software store will carry programs to help you write a resume, organize your job leads and contacts, and create your correspondence. Some packages are also designed to provide "career counseling," occupational information, or advice on your job search. Some of these programs are good and some are not. If such programs interest you, consider them–but remember that few people get job offers while playing with their computers. You *do* have to get interviews.

A new release from JIST, titled *America's Top Jobs™ on CD-ROM!* is an excellent resource for career exploration and job seeking. It includes all the descriptions from the *Occupational Outlook Handbook* plus another 7,700 more specialized jobs. And it's only $24.95! It's a good example of what can be done with good software.

More Good Books by Mike Farr

The Very Quick Job Search, 2nd Edition
Get a Better Job in Half the Time!

Selected as Best Self-Help Book of the Year!
2nd Edition! A thorough and well-done book presenting everything you need to know on career planning and job seeking.

$16.95
Order Code LP-J1812

The Quick Resume & Cover Letter Book, 2nd Edition
Write and Use an Effective Resume in Only One Day!

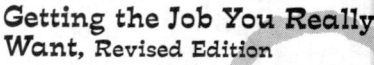

Voted as one of the top three business books of the year! Step-by-step advice plus many great examples.

$14.95
Order Code LP-J6342

The Quick Interview & Salary Negotiation Book
Dramatically Improve Your Interviewing Skills in Just a Few Hours!

This is THE comprehensive guide to improving your interview skills.

$14.95
Order Code LP-J1626

Getting the Job You Really Want, Revised Edition

This revised edition covers career planning and job seeking skills with lots of in-the-book worksheets and checklists. *Over 250,000 copies sold! Used in hundreds of job search programs across the country!*

$12.95
Order Code LP-RWR

America's Top Jobs® for College Graduates, 3rd Edition

Up-to-date descriptions of over 100 jobs most often held by college grads including pay and trends. PLUS: job search advice, employment outcomes by major, labor market trends, and more.

$16.95
Order Code LP-J4935

America's Top Jobs® for People Without a Four-Year Degree, 4th Edition

Thorough descriptions of 111 major jobs that don't require a four-year college degree. PLUS: lists of the fastest growing and best paying jobs and industries, job search advice, training and education options, and more.

$16.95
Order Code LP-J4900

3-1-01